VALUES IN SEXUALITY EDUCATION

A PHILOSOPHICAL STUDY

Ronald William Morris, Ph.D.
Department of Religion and Philosophy in Education
Faculty of Education
McGill University, Montreal

UNIVERSITY
PRESS OF
AMERICA

Lanham • New Yo

Copyright © 1994 by
University Press of America®, Inc.
4720 Boston Way
Lanham, Maryland 20706

3 Henrietta Street
London WC2E 8LU England

Library of Congress Cataloging-in-Publication Data

Morris, Ronald William.
Values in sexuality education : a philosophical study /
Ronald William Morris.
p.   cm.
Includes bibliographical references and index.
1. Sex instruction—History—20th century.   2. Sex instruction—
Moral and ethical aspects.   3. Sexology—Philosophy.   I. Title.
HQ56.M696   1994   306.7'07—dc20   94–11491 CIP

ISBN 0–8191–9556–1 (cloth : alk. paper)
ISBN 0–8191–9557–X (pbk. : alk. paper)

The paper used in this publication meets the minimum requirements of
American National Standard for Information Sciences—Permanence
of Paper for Printed Library Materials, ANSI Z39.48–1984.

This book is dedicated to the memory of André Guindon.

CONTENTS

TABLES

PREFACE

Whenever I observe a debate on values in sexuality education, whether it be in the media, in the literature, or in a gathering of educators and parents, I can usually identify two very distinct positions. The first position could be described as "suspicious." Here people immediately ask "whose values will be taught?" They worry that teachers might impose their own values. Parents will say: "I don't want just any teacher imposing *his* or *her* own values on *my* children." Some even worry that the school or teacher might attempt to *change* their children's values. They feel that families, and not schools, should teach values.

The second position is much more pro-school. Here people speak with great conviction of the need for sexuality education in the schools given the rate of unwanted teenage pregnancy and sexually transmitted diseases - especially AIDS. Recalling the inadequacy of their own sexuality education (one or two classes with a film on puberty), they see values as a vital component of a more comprehensive approach to sexuality education. They hope that a comprehensive approach will make existing programs and approaches more effective.

In response to those people who worry that teachers will arbitrarily impose their own values, those in favor of school based programs emphasize that one should not impose values but rather help young people *clarify* their values. The need to clarify values is usually justified on the basis that values are personal and subjective. This claim leaves proponents of the first position unsatisfied, and usually leads to accusations of relativism.

The one thing I rarely see in these debates is a critical examination of the assumptions underlying both positions. My first objective in writing this book is precisely to examine more closely our most influential presuppositions about values in sexuality education. My overall objective is to provide a framework for further discussion, exploration and development.

ACKNOWLEDGMENTS

I would like to express my deepest gratitude to William Lawlor for his valuable suggestions, his constant encouragement throughout the writing of this book, and for his wonderful sense of humor, hospitality and celebration. Special thanks to the late André Guindon for responding to the many drafts, and for his example of integrity and courage. Thanks to Elizabeth Wood for taking the time to proofread the manuscript amidst a very busy schedule, to my family, friends, and students who expressed their interest and encouragement, and to Howard Stutt, Rachelle Keyserlingk, Stanley Nemiroff, Joseph Hofbeck, Gerry McKay, David Smith, and Ted Wall for their support. Finally, my deepest gratitude to my mother for knowing the difference between "holding on" and "holding onto," to Madeleine for being there when it mattered most, and to Martin Jeffery for opening a whole world of possibility.

Credits:

Grateful acknowledgment is made for permission to reprint the following material:

Lines from "The Evolving Self: Problem and Process in Human Development," by Robert Kegan. Reprinted by permission of the publishers from THE EVOLVING SELF: PROBLEM AND PROCESS IN HUMAN DEVELOPMENT by Robert Kegan, Cambridge, Mass.: Harvard University Press, Copyright 1982 by the President and Fellows of Harvard College.

A section of this book has appeared previously, in slightly altered form, in the following publication: The Canadian Journal of Human Sexuality ("Teaching Values in Sexuality Education: From Value-Freedom to Neutrality and Beyond," Vol. 2, No. 2, 1993).

INTRODUCTION

There is no area of deliberate human behavior that lacks a moral dimension. The value questions are everywhere - in politics, in sex, in business, in the rearing of children, and in the realm of what one owes to one's self. (Maguire, 1978, p. xv)

1. Background and Problem

My first experience with a formal lesson on sexuality was as a senior high school student in the early seventies. Our school had a special sex education week in which the school nurse would visit all grade 10 and 11 classes. She would give a presentation on male and female anatomy, ovulation, conception and contraception. I remember being quite bored by the countless facts and clinical diagrams until she did something that was extremely unusual, especially in a Catholic school. She distributed a condom for each student to examine and manipulate. Most of us seemed rather uncomfortable. Some students appeared disgusted while others just giggled. Much to my surprise the nurse looked quite comfortable with the topic and with our response to the flabby instrument.

The nurse then asked if we had any questions. I will never forget that moment. Dead silence. It was a silence which may have lasted 30 seconds, but felt more like 30 minutes! Finally one courageous student raised his hand. "Miss," he asked, "now that you have shown us all this, does this mean that we can go out and do it?" "All right," I thought, "right on, yes, what a great question!" I could sense a fever of anticipation and excitement rising throughout the class. Although others might have had a different question, I sensed that we were all eager to hear her answer. For the first time, however, she seemed somewhat uncomfortable. This was her answer: "that's a really good question. But unfortunately I can't answer that. That's something you're going to have to decide for yourself. I suggest that you ask your parents when you get home." What a disappointment! Nothing! I don't think we expected her to come right out and say "yes" or "no," or to tell us what to do. We were hoping, however, that she would initiate some sort of discussion - especially since there was no way most of us could discuss this question with our parents.

The nurse's response to my classmate's question was consistent with the mentality and atmosphere of that period. In the sixties and seventies sexuality education was inspired by a positivistic paradigm. Teachers, it was argued, should avoid values and concentrate on facts validated by the scientific community (Karmel, 1970). Sexuality and education were seen in dualistic terms. It was assumed that facts and values were separate, and that education in sexuality, therefore, should deal separately with questions of value and questions of fact. The nurse, biology or physical education teacher would deal with the biology "part," and parents, or in some cases the religion teacher, would deal with the moral "part."

Although this dualism persists, the enthusiasm for a totally value-free sexuality education has begun to subside. Recognizing that sexuality involves more than biology, and that education is more than just information, sexuality educators throughout North America now acknowledge the importance of values. There is a growing conviction that school programs which deal only with the so-called "facts of life" are incomplete and ultimately ineffective (Barrett, 1990, 1991; Brick, 1985; Darling & Mabe, 1989; Desaulniers, 1982; Durand, 1985; Gordon, 1981; Gilgun & Gordon, 1983; Herold, 1984; Kenny & Orr, 1984; Lawlor, Morris, McKay, Purcell, & Comeau, 1990; Naus, 1989, 1991; Naus & Theis, 1991; Pegis, Gentles, & de Veber, 1986; Samson, 1979; 1981; Varcoe, 1988).

Empirical research in sexuality education has also begun to consider value-related issues. Survey research has thrown new light on views and perceptions of value issues (Lawlor et al., 1990, Lawlor & Purcell, 1989a, 1989b, 1990; Marsman & Herold, 1986; Morris, 1986, 1991). Experimental studies have attempted to measure the impact of school programs on knowledge, behavior and values (Kirby, 1980, 1985; Parcel, Luttman, & Flaherty-Zonis, 1985).

There have been, however, very few conceptual studies on values and sexuality education. The academic literature in sexuality education tends to focus more on technical and organizational questions than on substantive issues (Trudell, 1985).

Edmund Diori (1985) notes that philosophers of education, surprisingly, have had very little to say about the nature, parameters or goals of sexuality education.

> This lack of interest by philosophers in sex education is both surprising and disturbing. It is surprising because sex education commonly is assumed to be closely linked to moral education, which long has been of interest to educational philosophers. It is disturbing because the lack of philosophical attention only can facilitate the maintenance of doctrinaire, conventional assumptions about sex as foundations for sex education programs. (Diori, 1981, p. 225)

This lack of philosophical attention has meant that the field's most influential presuppositions have gone relatively unchallenged since the time of the school episode described above. In this book I examine two of those presuppositions. The first is the conceptualization of sexuality education as an object in the school curriculum designed to solve problems like teenage pregnancy and sexually transmitted diseases (Brick, 1987; Diori, 1985; Pegis, Gentles, & de Veber, 1986). I argue that this view of sexuality education is reductionistic and overly instrumental. It reduces education to schooling, sexuality to problems arising from coitus, and valuing to decision-making. It evaluates the success of sexuality education by strictly utilitarian criteria.

The second issue examined in the book is the widespread assumption that values are personal and subjective, and that teachers, therefore, ought to remain neutral (Bruess & Greenberg, 1981; Gordon, 1981; Harmin, Kirschenbaum, & Simon, 1973; Harmin 1988; Kelly, 1985; Morrison & Price, 1974; Pegis, Gentles & de Veber, 1986; Read, Simon, & Goodman, 1977; Varcoe, 1988). This thesis argues that value-neutrality is neither possible nor desirable. Although the commitment to neutrality is often based on an appreciation and respect for pluralism, on the subjective nature of values, and on the integrity of persons, it confuses pluralism with relativism, subjectivity with subjectives, and integrity with validity.

3. Outline

Part One of the book (chapters one to three) reviews and critiques the literature's understanding of the role and nature of values in sexuality education.

Chapter one situates the issues outlined above by examining values and sexuality education in historical perspective. It outlines how sexuality education has moved from a moralistic ethic to values clarification, neutrality and decision-making, and how the dominant paradigm has remained crisis oriented and instrumental.

Chapter two examines the presuppositions of the crisis-instrumental paradigm, the conviction that values are personal and subjective, and the issue of value-neutrality.

Chapter three presents Lawrence Kohlberg's theory of moral development and education. It outlines Kohlberg's critique of values clarification and examines whether Kohlberg's theory represents an adequate alternative. The latter part of the chapter examines Carol Gilligan's critique of Kohhlberg and points to the limitations of a formalistic ethic.

Part Two of the book (chapters four to six) proposes a more holistic view of sexual-values education.

Chapters four and five examine Robert Kegan's (1979; 1980; 1982) theory of human development. Chapter four delineates the basic tenets of the theory. Chapter five examines Kegan's stages and the "cultures of embeddedness" which, according to Kegan, enhance development throughout the life-span.

Chapter six examines the educational issues and principles arising. It examines what it means to teach values responsibly in light of Kegan's theory on the cultures of embeddedness, as well as the importance of narrative and storytelling for sexual-values education. Chapter six also outlines a preliminary sketch for a life-span view of sexual-values education.

Conn (1986) has used Kegan's stages as an empirical basis for a theory of moral and religious conversion. Guindon (1989a) has used the stages as a framework for a revisioned view of moral development, and to clarify the concept of the "fundamental option" in Catholic ethics (Guindon, 1990). In this book Kegan's theory, particularly his theory on the cultures of embeddedness, is used as a framework for reconceptualizing the meaning of sexual-values *education*; that is, for redefining the dominant assumptions about the nature, purpose, and organization of sexual-values education.

4. Usage and Meanings of the Term "Values"

The following definitions of the term "values" represent points of departure. I will return to the meanings of this term at various places in the book. Since one of my major objectives is to reconceptualize the understanding of "sexuality education" that presently dominates the literature, I will explore the meanings of the term sexuality education itself in subsequent chapters, particularly in the concluding chapter.

The term "*values*" will refer to *moral* values. "Moral," as Daniel Maguire (1978) argues, "means human in the ought or normative sense" (p. 114). When we say that rape is immoral, for example, "we are saying that it is an inhuman activity; that is not what humans' ought to do in expressing their sexuality" (p. 115). Sexual-moral values have an epistemological meaning. They name what is most human about sexuality (Guindon, 1989b). They are ideals or "standards of goodness or rightness" which serve as points of reference in evaluation, decision-making or action (Guindon, 1977, p. 22; cf. French, 1985, pp. 15-24). Moral "*valuing*" is the process by which we discern what is good or humanizing.

Moral values also represent our most fundamental convictions. Moral values run deeper than attitudes (Samson, 1987), and are more ontological than pragmatic. They define "what one will be, instead of merely what one will have" (Maguire, 1978, p. 94). Values at this level are not mere tools for decision-making. They do, however, orient or give meaning to human action (Desaulniers, 1982). As Maurice Friedman (1984) writes, real living values are "life stances that we embody and reveal in ever-new and unexpected ways" (p. 63).

PART ONE

REVIEW AND CRITIQUE OF THE LITERATURE'S PHILOSOPHICAL ORIENTATION ON VALUES IN SEXUALITY EDUCATION

CHAPTER 1

Values and Sexuality Education in Historical Perspective

This chapter outlines major trends in the history of North American views on sexuality education. It focuses on the organized campaigns for the inclusion of sexuality education in the school curriculum, as well as on popular and academic literature on sexuality education. The aim of the chapter is to place in historical perspective present views on values in sexuality education. An exhaustive treatment of the ways in which sexuality has been taught throughout history is beyond the scope of the chapter.[1]

1.1. The Late 19th and Early 20th Centuries

In the United States the first organized campaign for school-based sexuality education began in the 1890s. This campaign was rooted in two movements of the Progressive era: the scientific social hygiene and the purity movements (Trudell, 1985, p. 10). The purity movement was organized around a battle against prostitution. Its members called for greater public discourse on sexuality and emphasized "love and reproductive responsibility" over sexual commerce. They advocated a "moral education" where mothers would teach their children "the sanctities and the terrors of this awful power of sex, its capacities to bless or curse its owner" (cited in D'Emilio & Freedman, 1988, pp. 155, 156). Leadership in this movement came primarily from the "Protestant clergy, former abolitionists, and women's rights activists" (p. 150).

The scientific social hygiene movement was founded in 1905 by a physician named Prince Morrow.[2] Its major goal was to promote and develop an educational campaign that would curb the rate of sexually transmitted diseases. It sought to eliminate ignorance about sexuality, which, according to one writer, had "borne its monstrous brood of disease, misery, and moral degradation" (Gay, 1984, p. 318). The society spoke before medical associations, charitable organizations, women's clubs, and different professional associations. It was successful in obtaining the cooperation of organizations like the YMCA, "state boards of health, superintendents of schools, and teachers' organizations" (D'Emilio & Freedman, 1988, p. 205).

Under the rubric of "science" the hygiene movement of the early 20th century attempted to free sexuality from its Gnostic legacy. It continued, however, to perpetuate a dualistic and pessimistic view of sexuality. It firmly believed that "sex instruction should avoid detailed descriptions of external human anatomy." Instruction on sexuality, it was argued, "should aim to keep sex consciousness and sex emotions at a minimum, and should avoid everything which tends to awaken or to intensify either" (cited in Trudell, 1985, p. 12). The scientific hygiene movement represented "a return to Victorian middle class morality which sought to repress all nonprocreative sexual activity outside the family" (p. 12).

According to Schlossman and Wallach (1978), the main goals of the sex education movements in the early part of the 20th century were to:

> purify discourse on sex, particularly in the popular press and among children, and to instill moral inhibitions against sexual gratification now that effective birth control and cures for venereal disease were becoming widely available. The sex educators were moral crusaders marching under the banner of medical and pedagogical science. They sought to develop instructional techniques for innocently conveying new medical knowledge about sex to children, and, at the same time, imbuing sex with older spiritual meanings. Sex education was a means of pedagogical warfare against the purveyors of sexual titillations. Far from encouraging freer discussion of sex, the sex educators wanted to discipline lust and channel it to conventional moral ends. (p. 226)

Meanwhile in Canada Arthur Beall was hired by the Ontario Ministry of Education to give lectures on eugenics and personal hygiene

(Barrett, 1990).   In the year 1900, responding to a request by the Women's Christian Temperance Union, Beall became Canada's official "agent of purity" (Monk, 1984). He lectured both male and female secondary students on the evils of cigarette smoking, kissing, obscene pictures and stories. He warned boys of the tragic consequences of losing one's "vital fluids." These fluids, claimed Beall, are produced by the "glands of life" whose role is to nourish the brain and nervous system. Masturbation was seen as particularly dangerous. It could lead to insanity, something that was considered much worse than death (Monk, 1984).

A series of books for young men and women became very popular in the United States and Canada at the same time that Beall was giving his lectures. An eight volume series called "Self and Sex" by Sylvanus Stall, a Lutheran pastor and Doctor of Divinity, was written especially for men. Young women were encouraged to read "What a Young Girl Ought to Know" by Mary Wood-Allen, a physician and member of the Women's Christian Temperance Union (Monk, 1984). Like many of the manuals discussed above, these books were highly prescriptive and were based on numerous biological misconceptions. According to Peter Gay (1984), "the purpose of Dr. Wood-Allen's books, like that of Dr. Stall's, was to preserve purity, which is to say, to prevent pollution. The pessimism of this literature about human nature is almost unrelieved" (p. 323).

The goals of the sexuality education movements of this period were informed by a proliferation of medical advice literature warning men and women about the perils of non-marital and non-procreative sexual behavior. Most of the literature for men focused on the dangers of masturbation. Benjamin Rush, who is known as the father of American Psychiatry, warned young men that masturbation:

> produces seminal weakness, impotence, dysury, tabes dorsalis, pulmonary consumption, dyspepsia, dimness of sight, vertigo, epilepsy, hypochondriasis, loss of memory, managlia, fatuity, and death . . . It reduces the patient to a state of stupidity. Neither plague nor war, nor small pox, nor crowd of similar evils, have resulted more disastrously for humanity than the habit of masturbation: it is the destroying element of civilized society. (cited in Szasz, 1980, pp. 17-18)

In 1857 an English physician, Dr. William Acton, published a book on reproduction which became very popular in France and the United States. Like most of the medical literature of this time, it focused almost exclusively on sexual disorders. Nocturnal emissions were seen as a form of "pollution." Acton wrote that masturbation leads to apathy, loss of self-reliance, impulsivity, irritability, incoherence of language, and among other things, "chronic dementia." Young men, he advised, should do everything they can to "constipate" their genitals (Marcus, 1985, pp. 12-25).

Acton's book had little to say about the reproductive biology of women. He did, however, offer some prescriptions and reflections on women and sexual desire. "The majority of women (happily for society)," wrote Acton, "are not very much troubled with sexual feelings of any kind. . . Love of home, of children, and of domestic duties are the only passions they feel" (cited in D'Emilio & Freedman, 1988, p. 70). To "stifle" the sexual desire of women, Acton recommended a regular regimen of pregnancy and childbearing. "If the married female conceives every second year, during the nine months that follow conception she experiences no great sexual excitement" (cited in Marcus, 1985, p. 30).

Along with the proliferation of medical advice literature, physicians collaborated in the development of numerous devices designed to prevent nocturnal emissions and masturbation. A popular device for men was a penile ring with nails protruding inwards, and a "spermatorrhea ring" that would send an electric shock during an erection (Greenland, 1974). Seen from the perspective of the late 20th century, these gadgets appear somewhat bizarre and amusing. But for the physicians of the early part of the century, prevention of "pollution" was serious business. Describing the effectiveness of the "spermatorrhea ring," J. L. Milton, a prominent English surgeon, wrote:

> The reader must have seen the effects of this little instrument to appreciate its value . . . The first patient I treated with it was the worst I ever saw. A remarkable strong built man, he looked the very picture of despondency . . . The emissions yielded with extraordinary rapidity, and at the expiration of quite seven or eight years, had never returned. Since then I have employed it in hundreds of cases. (cited in Greenland, 1974, p. 8)

Similar advice was given by Catholic theologians, although the solution for nocturnal emissions was less spectacular. In the late 1920's Kirsch, for example, advised young people not to intentionally cause nocturnal emissions. "Although you cannot help feeling the pleasure if you awake," wrote Kirsch, "you must not surrender yourself to the pleasure." His main advice was: "try to think of something else, forget about the emission, say a Hail Mary, and turn over and go to sleep" (cited in Kirkendall, 1981, p. 6).

1.2. The 1960s and Early 70s

The next major period in the history of North American sexuality education begins in the 1960s (Trudell, 1985). The first issue of the Sex Information and Education Council of Canada (SIECCAN) was published in 1966 (Barrett, 1990). The Sex Information and Education Council of the United States (SIECUS) was founded in 1964. The founding members of SIECUS consisted of a physician, an educator, a minister, a business executive, and an attorney. According to Lester Kirkendall (1981), one of SIECUS's founding members, the organization chose to "take the broadest possible view of sexuality" (p. 7). Although SIECUS (1970) recognized that values plays an important role in sex education, it attempted to situate sexuality in a scientific framework. The following excerpt of an interview with Mary Calderone, a founding member of SIECUS, clearly articulates this perspective.

> HH: As I recall it, your original purpose was to link sex with health.
> Dr. C: Yes, and that turned out to be wise because it took sex out of the realm of morals. Fundamentally, sex has always been preempted by the religions and everybody kept hands off. By putting it into the area of health, where it scientifically belongs, by recognizing its role in physical, mental, and social well-being, we immediately freed it up for objective, less emotional study and considerations. (cited in Szasz, 1980, p. 122)

Some social scientists in this period argued that sexuality education should remain value-free. Louis Karmel (1970), for example, argued that sexuality education should be limited to "sex information." This information should impart "biological and mechanistic data without prescribing how these impulses should or should not be channeled" (p.95). Karmel saw the teaching of value-related areas as inappropriate for public schools given the growing pluralism of American society and given the lack of certainty about value issues. He suggested that "schools need to give `sexual facts' which are established as valid in the scientific community," and these facts should be presented "without value judgments" (p. 95). "What schools need to do is to treat sex as they would treat digestion, no more, no less." They should limit themselves to information about "conception, gestation, birth, and nursing" (p. 96).

Karmel suggested that teachers "be selected and trained by competent behavioral scientists" to ensure that value judgments would not be made in the classroom. He reasoned that if children are exposed to value-free information "they will be in a position to make their own ethical judgments" (p. 96).

The development of sexuality education in this period met with considerable opposition. The most visible and vocal opposition came from right wing political and religious organizations such as The John Birch Society, Mothers for Moral Stability (MOM), and Parents for Orthodoxy in Parochial Schools (POPE) (Monk, 1984). These groups vociferously attacked all forms of school based programs. Supporters of sexuality education were called corrupters of youth, communists, atheists, child molesters and rapists (see for example: Drake, 1969; Lentz, 1972). In Canada, opponents of sexuality education claimed that programs were being supported by the drug industry and that the content of these programs was determined by atheists and communists. They argued that sexuality education in the schools would lead to moral perversion and a disintegration of the family (Monk, 1984).

1.3. From the 1970s to the Present

In spite of continued opposition, this period is marked by growing support for sexuality education in the school. Surveys in Canada (Gallup, 1984; Lawlor & Purcell, 1989a, 1989b; Marsman & Herold, 1986; Monk, 1984; Nolte, 1984; Lawlor, Morris, McKay, Purcell & Comeau, 1990) and in the United States (Alexander, 1984; Kenney & Orr, 1984; Sexuality Education, 1990) all indicate that most parents, students, and teachers see sexuality education as both valid and necessary. As Peggy Brick (1987) writes: "research consistently demonstrates widespread public, and particularly parental, support for sex education" (p. 5).

This support is also marked by a growing consensus on the importance of addressing values in school-based programs. By the 1980s, any remaining enthusiasm for a value-free sexuality education has largely evaporated. Despite the appeal of the positivistic paradigm, we see a growing conviction that school proprams which deal only with the "facts of life" are ultimately unsatisfactory (Morris, 1993).

In Quebec, for example, the Ministry of Education (1985) has developed a sexuality education program which states that: "because it is linked with the person and with human behavior, because it is the subject of a moral position in every society, because it holds the attention of all religions, sex education may not be given without reference to values" (p. 103).

In the United States, an emphasis on values can also be found among groups promoting a comprehensive approach to sexuality education. In a recent update of its position, for example, SIECUS (SIECUS Position, 1990) has spoken of the need for *sexuality* education, as opposed to mere *sex* education which is what most of the literature had been referring to until then. They argue that "human sexuality encompasses sexual knowledge, beliefs, attitudes, values, and behaviors" and deals with "ethical, spiritual, and moral concerns..." A comprehensive sexuality education, therefore, addresses:

> the biological, sociocultural, psychological, and spiritual dimensions of sexuality from 1) the cognitive domain (facts, data, and information; 2) the affective domain (feelings, values, and attitudes; and 3) the behavioral domain (the skills to communicate effectively and to make responsible decisions). (p. 10)

Some sexuality educators argue that programs should be based on clearly identifiable values. They argue that presenting or "proposing" values will assist in the decision-making process (Calderone & Johnson, 1989; Desaulniers, 1981, 1982; Dickman, 1982; Gilgun & Gordon, 1983; Scales, 1984; Tatum, 1981). Although a positivistic framework had been present in much of the sexuality education during the sixties and seventies, a values-based approach was, by the late sixties, being advocated by Rubin (1968) who argued that moral values provide "a kind of road map" for students. His position on the nature and source of these values is characteristic of those who espouse this perspective.

There are common values that are basic to a democratic society and
that most thoughtful persons will agree upon regardless of their
different beliefs: 1) respect for the basic worth, equality and dignity
of each individual; 2) accordance of the right of self-determination
to each human being; 3) recognition of the need for cooperative
effort for the common good; and 4) respect for truth. (p. 114)

Sol Gordon (1981) has argued that specific values can be presented
in a non-indoctrinating way if they are based on American democracy.
"Sex education as moral education would foster the basic values
embodied in the constitution and the Bill of Rights. Since America is a
democratic society, and public schools are committed to these values,
this type of education is logical and appropriate for American society"
(p. 29). According to Calderone & Johnson (1989), the task is to outline
basic values which "should be acceptable to any community in our
American democracy" (p. 200).

In Quebec the ministry of education also favors this approach
(Durand, 1985). The program designed by the ministry lists a series of
values such as "love of life," "respect for one's body," "respect for the
person of others, regardless of their physical characteristics and sexual
orientations," and "the equality of each person, regardless of his/her
sex." The list of values is proposed not as dogma but as "one example
of values linked with sex education and chosen by a particular society:
the society of Quebec" (Desaulniers, 1982, p. 318).

This view of values represents a significant development in sexuality
education. It recognizes that fact and value are inseparable. Explicitly
identifying one's values is much more likely to encourage objectivity
since one's most influential presuppositions become accessible and
thereby subject to criticism, dialogue and revision.

In spite of the emergence of this perspective on values, the
commitment to value-freedom and neutrality persists through the 1980s.
The idea that sexuality education ought to remain value-free can be
found in those authors, like Karmel above, who are committed to the
positivistic ethic which says that facts and values ought to remain
separate (Kelly, 1988). It can also be found among educators who fear
controversy or accusations of preaching and moralizing. The following
quotation, taken from the introduction to a recent book on safer sex and
condoms, is a perfect example. Although the authors refer to value-
ladden concepts such as wisdom, responsibility, procreation, pleasure,
and intimacy, they begin their introduction with the claim that their book

is a-moral, a claim which is supposed to reassure the reader. The narrators of this introduction are male and female sexual organs.

> This presentation has nothing to do with morals or religious beliefs. Instead, it is an expression of our desire to increase knowledge and create a climate of understanding. It is an attempt to help you so that you will use us wisely and responsibly. We are sexual organs whose sole function are to procreate and give pleasure. We are one way of enjoying intimate contact with others. (Arioli & Blake, 1987, p. 1)[3]

The commitment to value-neutrality is most consistently found among proponents of values clarification. Although proponents of values clarification reject the idea that sexuality education should be value-*free*, they do argue that teachers should remain value-*neutral*. They argue that teachers should be non-judgmental and should convey to students that there are no right or wrong answers. Since values are viewed as personal and subjective, the teacher's role is to ex-pose but not im-pose values. Sexuality education, the argument goes, ought to encourage decision-making by helping students *clarify* their *own* values. This is by far the most popular position on values in sexuality education (Breckon & Sweeney, 1978; Bruess & Greenberg, 1981; Harmin, Kirschenbaum & Simon, 1973; Harmin, 1988; Kirschenbaum, 1977; Morrison & Price, 1974; Parcel & Gordon, 1981; Power, 1980; Raths, Harmin & Simon, 1978; Read, Simon & Goodman, 1977; Varcoe, 1988).[4]

Like most popular movements in education, values clarification has recently come under considerable attack (Kelly, 1988, p. 288; Knapp, 1981). Some critics argue that values clarification is pedagogically destructive, promotes ethical relativism, undermines the authority of parents, and is a sign of moral decline (Bloom, 1987; Boyd & Bogdan, 1984; Gabler & Gabler, 1987; Gow, 1980).

Others argue that values clarification masks a conspiracy against traditional moral and religious values. Phyllis Schlafly (1983), for example, argues that values clarification is an attempt to "change the students' values and attitudes rather than the traditional purpose to impart knowledge" (p. 47). According to Schlafly, values clarification is part of a larger scheme "to teach teenagers (and sometimes children) how to enjoy fornication without having a baby and without feeling guilty" (p. 46). Critics like Schlafly go as far as to say that modern attempts at sexuality education promote "promiscuity" and are the major cause of teenage pregnancy (cf. Richert, 1983).[5] These criticisms are part of larger reactionary movement against all forms of sexuality education which fail to propose abstinence-only curricula (Sedway, 1992).

Values clarification, and particularly its commitment to neutrality, persists in spite of (and perhaps even because of) these scathing criticisms. The literature on sexuality education consistently affirms that "values are personal and subjective" and almost always equate the terms "values" and "valuing" with "clarification" (for example: George & Behrendt, 1985, p. 57; Kelly, 1988, p. 290; Herold, 1984, p. 162). "Clarity of values" is even used as the measure of values and valuing in research on the effectiveness of school-based programs (Kirby, 1985; Parcel, Luttman, & Flaherty-Zonis, 1985).

In an article on values in sexuality education, Varcoe (1988) argues that school programs need to promote values clarification. Conscious of the accusation that values clarification attempts to change values, Varcoe suggests that programs should clarify existing values rather than instill new ones. "New values," says Varcoe, "need not be taught, just existing values brought to the surface and clarified" (p. 161).

Varcoe's perspective is part of the long standing tradition which sees sexuality education as a solution to sexual-moral problems. Values clarification is now seen as the missing link between information and responsible behavior. "Once values clarification is part of every sex education curriculum the number of teenage pregnancies and sexually transmitted diseases should decrease" (Varcoe, 1988, p. 161). The following chapter examines the assumptions underlying this claim, as well as the presuppositions underlying the commitment to value neutrality.

NOTES:

1. Sexuality education is as old as the species. A complete history of sexuality education would tell the story of the explicit and implicit ways in which sexual information, attitudes, values, and behaviors have been taught and learned from time immemorial. More recently, it would be a history of how sexuality has been shaped by social institutions such as the family, modern medicine, churches, the criminal justice system, and schools. It would identify the changing structures, power relations, rules, regulations, policies, rituals,

relations, architectural layouts, interests, and requirements influencing and governing sexual values and behaviors in these institutions. A complete history of sexuality education would examine how different historical developments are linked to changes (or lack of change) in the status of men and women, economic conditions and ethos, the growing influence of the mass media (especially television), literacy, urbanization, and the impact of social and political movements like feminism.

A complete history of sexuality education would also explore the history of silence on sexual matters. According to Michel Foucault (1980), silence actually represents a "regime of discourses." There are many types of silence which form an "integral part of the strategies that underlie and permeate discourses" (p. 27). On the surface, for example, it appears as though European secondary schools of the eighteenth century had no sexuality education. Very little was said about sexuality in a formal sense. But according to Foucault: "one only has to glance over the architectural layout, the rules of discipline, and their whole internal organization: the question of sex was a constant preoccupation... The spaces for classes, the shape of the tables, the planning of the recreation lessons, the distribution of dormitories (with or without partitions, with or without curtains), the rules for monitoring bedtime and sleep periods - all this referred in the most prolix manner, to the sexuality of children" (p. 28).

2. Societies with similar objectives and approaches were founded in Europe (Gay, 1984, pp. 318-320).

3. It is this type of contradiction which raises the ire of right-wing political and religious organizations. Although these organizations often level outrageous and unfounded accusations against proponents of sexuality education, they are accurate in their perception that what is being preached, as Moran (1989) writes, "conflicts with what they are preaching" (p. 172).

4. My colleagues and I found that most teachers of sexuality education in the Montreal area favor values clarification and its ethic of neutrality (Lawlor, Morris, McKay, Purcell & Comeau, 1990; Morris, 1986).

5. In Quebec, similar viewpoints have been expressed by the Association of Catholic Parents (Desaulniers, 1981, 1982).

CHAPTER 2

The Crisis-Instrumental Paradigm and The Ethic of Value-Neutrality

2.1. The Assumptions of a Crisis-Instrumental Paradigm

The increasing rate of teenage pregnancies and STDs have consistently served as the justification for school-based sexuality education. As a result, the value of school programs have been measured by their ability to reduce the rates of pregnancy and disease among young people (Kirby, 1983; Barrett, 1990). When new techniques and approaches are introduced, they are done so in the hope of making school programs more effective. Varcoe's (1988) views on values clarification is a good example. As was seen in the previous chapter, she argues that "once values clarification is part of every sex education curriculum, the number of teenage pregnancies and sexually transmitted diseases should decrease" (p. 161).

After a four year study, Kenniston and the Carnegie Council on children (1977) concluded that poverty, unemployment, and discrimination were the chief problems facing children in North America. It is now estimated that one fifth of American children live in poverty (Scheller, 1991). The perspective represented by Varcoe (1988) assumes that something magical, independent of these conditions, will occur once students have clarified their values. Any approach to sexuality education which sees school programs as a solution to problems like unwanted teenage pregnancy fails to consider the objective conditions which perpetuate these "problems." As Trudell (1985) writes:

Once the "problem" has been defined individually, the "solution" becomes changing certain characteristics via education, rather than changing larger social or economic factors that might be involved. For example, focusing on the percentage of out-of-wedlock birth to black teens, 55% in 1979, compared to 9.3% for white teens, obscures the role of cultural differences in the meaning of this event to a black teenager as well as economic inequities such as higher unemployment and lower average wages for blacks. We might well ask whether it is these systematic conditions of economic discrimination or instead teenage pregnancy that represents the larger problem for the black community. (p. 13)

It is extremely difficult to change behavior through school programs. As Peter Naus (1991) explains, behaviors are solidly entrenched and sustained by social and economic structures and practices. Behaviors are not likely to change as long as these structures and practices remain in place (p. 12; cf. Naus, 1989; Naus & Theis, 1991). Classroom techniques are important. It is unrealistic, however, to believe that techniques will somehow "fix" the problem.

The reliance on classroom techniques to solve problems like STDs (or drugs, violence, and illiteracy) assumes that education is something that occurs primarily, if not exclusively, in school classrooms.[1] It places an extraordinary burden on teachers (Moran, 1987, p. 11), and obscures the educational role and responsibilities of the school as a whole, of families, the work place, the mass media, the business world, and the state. It is important to recognize that:

schools can never provide a full education in human sexuality; we are expecting too much of teachers if we ask them to take on a responsibility that the rest of the community has avoided, to solve a problem that the whole of society has created. (Jackson, 1982, p. 160)

The conceptualization of sexuality education as a form of crisis-intervention is largely based on the taken-for-granted assumption that pregnancy rates reveal a "crisis" of adolescent sexuality. A closer look, however, indicates that these rates contain the same "statistical delusion" as modern divorce rates.[2] In the year 1850 the average young person began puberty at 16 or 17 years of age. The earliest recorded age was

12 years. Young people were married, on average, at 18 or 19 years of age. Adolescents, therefore, were sexually mature and unmarried for an average of 2 to 4 years, except for a few where this period lasted up to 7 years. In 1985 it would appear that puberty began, on average, at 12 or 13 years of age. The earliest age dropped to 8 years, while the average age for marriage was 22 to 23 years of age. "Adolescence," therefore, extended from 2 to 4 years in 1850 to an average of 11 years in 1985. In the 1980s this period could extend to as much as 15 years for those who began puberty earlier (Stayton, 1985).

The "problem" or "crisis" of adolescent sexuality is not so much that the rates of pregnancy are increasing. Rather, the problem is that teenagers in the eighties and nineties are expected to abstain from sexual activity, postpone pregnancy, and avoid STDs for a much longer period than ever before, and this with very few guidelines and with very little support.

The preoccupation with disease and pregnancy has led to a sexuality education which constantly tells young people what is bad about sexuality but rarely what is good and positive. The advent of AIDS has reinforced and intensified this view (Brick, 1987). As Bollerund, Christopherson and Frank (1990) indicate, "this lack of a positive standard leaves adolescents without guidance in making decisions, beyond the injunction to `just say no' to sex" (p. 282).

According to Robert Coles (1990), we have responded to the so-called "problem" of teen-age pregnancy with a condescending and patronizing attitude which consigns young women "to the ranks of a moral Lumpenproletariat." We offer sex education to young people "who are (they will say so over and over again) lost, bewildered, desperately hungry - sometimes literally so, but always spiritually so: for a sense of purpose and meaning in life, for something (for someone) to believe in, for moral direction . . ." (p. 97).

Castigating the "just say no" approaches to drugs, Neil Postman (1989) asks a question that has yet to show up in sexuality education: "How will we help [young people] find out what they need to say yes to?" (p. 124). Although values clarification seems to offer something beyond `just say no,' it still faces the same fundamental problem. Who will help young people to discover *what values* they need to clarify and live their lives by? How can they "be helped to read, and write, a coherent story for our times?" (p. 81). Paraphrasing Postman, one could argue that unless we help our students discover a purpose, unless we help them construct a meaningful story, the rates of teenage pregnancy and STDs are likely to remain high, not because teenagers will have failed to clarify their values, but 'because it won't make any difference if they do.' "Each person must find in the educational process something beyond learning the penmanship and grammar of his culture that gives him a name, a place, a passion, and story" (Keen, 1970, p. 124).[3]

The problem here is even more fundamental than the absence of guidelines for decision-making. The issues raised by Coles and Postman call into question the conceptualization of valuing as a form of decision-making. Ethicist Stanley Hauerwas (1980) argues that an ethic of "decision-making" assumes that the primary moral question is "What should I do?" rather than "What should I be?" The question "What should I do?" "masks a deep despair about the possibility of moral growth as it accepts us as we are. The only sign of hope such a view entertains is that we can free ourselves from who we are by making moral decisions . . ." Like Postman and Keen, Hauerwas argues that what is needed "is a narrative that gives us the ability to be what we are and yet go on" (pp. 476-477).

Gabriel Moran (1989) notes that "the phrase decision-making has become so much part of our language that people are often unaware they use it and how their lives may be distorted by the effort to make decisions, instead of simply deciding or letting decisions emerge" (p. 22). This observation is particularly relevant for sexuality education. The phrase "decision-making" has become so much part of the sexuality education vocabulary that researchers and teachers are often unaware of how classroom teaching may be distorted by the effort to promote decision-making. A closer look at the roots of this objective will reveal some of these distortions.

The reduction of values and valuing to decision-making is rooted in the modern Western image of self as "maker." In The *Human Condition* Hannah Arendt (1958) explains that the elimination of contemplation in favor of 'making' and 'doing' "from the range of meaningful human capacities," (p. 305) is "perhaps the most momentous of the spiritual consequences of the discoveries of the modern age" (p. 289). Prior to the modern age, as far back as Plato and Aristotle, contemplation and being were given primacy over making and doing. Truth was seen as something given and revealed in the stillness and receptivity of contemplation. In modern times - with the rise of science, industrialization and technology - knowledge and truth are seen in much more pragmatic terms. Humans can only know what they themselves make (p. 17). The modern person is *homo faber*, a maker and fabricator.

In the following passage Arendt summarizes the main attitudes of *homo faber*:

> his instrumentalization of the world, his confidence in tools and in the productivity of the maker of artificial objects; his trust in the all comprehensive range of the means-end category, his conviction that every issue can be solved and every human motivation reduced to the principle of utility; his sovereignty, which regards everything given as material and thinks of the whole of nature as of an immense fabric from which we can cut out whatever we want to resew it however we like; his equation of intelligence with ingenuity, that is, his contempt for all thought which cannot be considered to be "the first step...; finally his matter-of-course identification of fabrication with action. (pp. 305-306)

The present ecological crisis is, to a large extent, rooted in the appropriation and institutionalization of *homo faber*. Subscribing to the image of self-as-maker gives us the illusion that we are somehow in control, that we can make whatever we wish to satisfy our needs and interests. It renders meaningless the idea of life as gift, that is, the idea that humans receive rather than manufacture life, a vision which would call us to live as recipients in humble relationship to (rather than in dominion over) others and the environment. *Homo faber*, as Keen (1969) puts it, "has become a `waste maker,' the anus of the machine rather than its brain" (p. 125).

Homo faber is based exclusively on a masculine view of the world. The image of man-the-maker rests on the view that a "strong man" is someone who is "isolated against others," and who "owes his strength to his being alone" (Arendt, 1958, p. 188). *Homo faber* is "so exclusively `masculine,' writes Keen (1969), "that it makes impossible an appreciation of the dignity of the more `feminine' modes of perceiving and relating to the world" (p. 146).

An education based on the image of self-as-maker sees very little value in meditative attitudes like wonder, gratitude, celebration, silence, and receptivity (Keen, 1970, p. 43; Palmer, 1983, pp. 79-83, 117-121). Although "making," much like speaking and debating, is an appropriate and even necessary human activity, students also need opportunities to cultivate "an inner silence . . . an ability to let things happen, to welcome, to listen, to allow, to be at ease in situations in which surrender rather than striving for control is appropriate" (Keen. 1970, p. 43).

Gratitude is a fundamental component of responsibility. We are less likely to feel compassion for others if we are convinced that who we have become is the direct result of our own making. If, on the other hand, we see ourselves as humble recipients, as fortunate to be who we are, and to have what we have, then we allow ourselves to be moved by the plight of others. "We might feel obliged," as Palmer (1990) says, "to pass the gifts along rather than hoard our treasures to ourselves" (pp. 50-51). "Only enjoyment and gratitude for our lives create a spontaneous impulse to care for others" (Keen, 1991, p. 171). In a culture dominated by images of "man-the-maker," the more we have reasons to be grateful, the less grateful we actually are. *Homo faber* breeds moral numbness.

2.2. The Consequences of a Crisis-Instrumental Paradigm

In *Wisdom and the Senses* Joan Erikson (1988) tells a simple story that beautifully illustrates the modern preoccupation with making and doing.

> I watched two youngsters on the beach recently, one toddler just up on his feet and not too steady, the other a bit older with a wider range of skills... The toddler was wholly preoccupied with discovering sand. He caressed it, let it run through his fingers, tried it out with his toes, wiggled in it, and poured it on his tummy, completely absorbed. Then along came his mother with a toy truck and urged him to fill it with sand, suggesting as well that he should use a small shovel to build a castle. He complied half-heartedly and then crawled away, again exploring and testing. His mother tried again, so eager to have a purposeful son achieving, constructing, or at least to have these appropriate toys she had supplied brought into the act. (pp. 22-23)

This small episode is only one among many which "remind us that we live in a nontactile, predominantly kinesthetically dull, success-ridden society." We fail to appreciate the life and vitality that comes "with just being, enjoying the present moment" and living sensually "in a delight-giving space" (p. 23). The popular expression "time is money" is symptomatic of this failure. In Western culture time is always *for* something: making friends, making a deal, making love, making a living, making money. Persons who spend time doing nothing in particular, without any immediate goal, are seen to waist their time. In fact time is an enemy. If we suddenly find ourselves with unexpected free time we must quickly find something to do, we must fill the void. If we have unearned free time we must "kill" it (Keen, 1969, p. 144).

It is interesting that even meditation and relaxation are usually justified by their utilitarian value (Benson, 1975). We should meditate because meditation is an effective technique *for* reducing stress, improving one's performance, or increasing one's creative potential. There is no appreciation of the possibility that doing *nothing* may actually be *something* even though doing that something may be *for* nothing in particular. In other words, it is extremely difficult to revel in the vitality of just *being* in a culture that defines the human primarily as *maker* and human action as *instrumental*.

Similarly, it is difficult to celebrate the value of sexuality itself (Desaulnier, 1982), or to affirm the qualities of being fully alive as sexual beings, in an educational paradigm that reduces values to tools for making decisions about sexual-moral problems. The main focus of attention in a crisis-instrumental-mentality is not pleasure, joy, playfulness, intimacy, tenderness, sensuality, or the experience of *being in* relationship and being in love, but problems associated with *having sex* and *having relationships*.[4]

In an exceptional interview conducted by Roy Bonisteel (1980), Sondra Diamond describes how she was discouraged to pursue a college education because of her cerebral palsy. Her high school advisor reasoned that she would not really be able to do anything with a college degree. Sondra had considerable difficulty convincing him and others that her desire to learn was valid in itself. In a remarkable passage she also describes how science has yet to develop sophisticated enough instruments to measure humanness and how a child who experiences simple delights like the sensation of bed sheets on his or her skin is in fact knowing life. Sondra's whole life has been a struggle against a utilitarian and instrumental view of education and life. Her main challenge has not been "making decisions" but with finding a space to celebrate, in the words of Erikson (1988), the vitality that comes "with just being" and "enjoying the present moment" (p. 23).

The irony of a crisis-instrumental mentality is that it perpetuates the very problems it seeks to avoid. There is evidence which suggests that persons with a positive view of sexuality are much more likely to use contraception or to practice safer sex (Byrne & Fisher, 1983). Repeatedly telling young people that sexuality is dangerous and that

sexuality is a source of problems is not likely to cultivate a positive view
of sexuality.

A sexuality education which focuses almost exclusively on teenage
pregnancy and STDs allows, as Diori (1985) argues, the kinds of
behaviors which can lead to pregnancy and disease "to dominate the
total conception of sex itself" (p. 242).

> Any sex education program which approaches sex as inherently
> constituted by heterosexual copulation is likely to contribute to the
> tendency on the part of students to see it in that way. Sex educators
> whose primary concern is with preventing adolescent pregnancy,
> but whose programs further a conceptualization of sex as
> heterosexual copulation, risk promoting the very type of behavior
> which can result in pregnancy. (p. 247)

In a crisis paradigm students are given only two options. They are
told either to postpone their sexual "involvement"[5] or to use
contraception if they do decide to have sex. They are rarely, if ever,
invited to consider other sexual gestures besides coitus. If we really
want to prevent unwanted pregnancy and STDs, does it not make sense,
as Stevi Jackson (1982) asks, "to tell girls about the sensual potential of
their bodies, and let both boys and girls know that it is possible to give
and receive sexual pleasure without engaging in the act of intercourse"
(p. 152)? Unfortunately, this alternative "is ignored almost totally in the
sex education literature" because non-coital gestures "simply are not
seen as real sex" (Diori, 1985, p. 248; cf. Jackson, 1982, p. 118; Masters
& Johnson, 1975, pp. 253-255).

Advocates of abstinence might argue that teenagers ought to avoid
all sexual gestures because it is difficult to stop and not go "all the way."
Could the problem be that young people will go "all the way," not
because they can not stop once they have started, but because they have
appropriated the cultural myth which says that playful non-coital touch
is nothing more than foreplay, a prelude to the real thing? Could the real
challenge of sexuality education be to find ways of de-constructing the
myth of coitus?

Teaching as if coitus was the only sexual gesture worthy of concern
obscures the needs of those students who are not coitally active or who
may be concerned with more "mundane" and less "problematic"
experiences such as dating, holding hands and kissing. According to the
findings of a recent Canada wide study, this may represent the majority

of high school students in Canada. The researchers found that "at least 12 percent of males and eight percent of females" in grade 7 (12 years of age) experienced "sexual intercourse at least once" (King et al., 1988, p. 84). In grade 11 (16 years of age) 49 percent of males and 46 percent of females had experienced sexual intercourse. Although the study shows that many teenagers are coitally active, the study also indicates that approximately 90 percent of grade 7 students and over 50 percent of grade 11 students in Canada never have had coitus. Furthermore, only 3 percent of the 14-year-olds and 7 percent of 15-year-olds "had often had sexual intercourse" (p. 98).

It may well be that young people are growing tired of the crisis mentality. It is not unreasonable to assume that many young people will reject an educational orientation that constantly presents a distorted view of sexuality (Brick, 1987, p. 7). Based on numerous visits to high school sex education classes, and based on the feedback I receive from student teachers, I suspect that teenagers are increasingly frustrated with adults who, in the words of André Guindon (1987), "project their sexual poverty on young people."

This issue was recently addressed by a high school student in Montreal. Responding to an invitation by the editor of a major Montreal daily newspaper, Marie-Anne Legault wrote an article expressing her frustration with sex education in the schools. School programs, she wrote, present sexuality as an "infectious monster" to be avoided "at all costs."

> Obviously there are always exceptions, but most young people who are assuming their sexuality are seeking affection, tenderness, and love... we "young people" would have appreciated courses that were much more human and much less "mechanical"!!! (Legault, 1990, p. A20) [free translation]

Thus far I have referred almost exclusively to "young people." This is primarily because a crisis-instrumental-paradigm has nothing really meaningful or positive to offer the mentally or physically disabled, the terminally ill, the middle aged, the elderly or the dying. By reducing sexuality to coitus and valuing to decision-making, a crisis orientation has little to say about those persons who are not perceived as coitally active or as decision-makers. Aging, illness and death are seen to be about powerlessness, dependency and decline. They represent a threat to the potency and self-sufficiency of *homo-faber*. They are kept out of sight and out of mind because they are "evidence of the failure to control" (Keen, 1969, p. 130), and because they remind us of "the fragility of all our efforts at making" (Palmer, 1990, p. 51; cf. Calderone & Johnson, 1989; Nelson, 1978).

2.3. Values Clarification and the Idea that Values are Personal and Subjective

As was seen in the previous chapter, Values Clarification is one of the most popular approaches to values in sexuality education. Its proponents argue that values are personal and subjective, and that teachers, therefore, should abstain from value-judgments. Recall that although proponents of Values Clarification reject the idea that education should be value-free, they do argue that teachers ought to remain value-neutral. Value-neutrality is seen as safeguard against subjective biases, and against the arbitrary imposition of values.

It is important to emphasize that this idea is not limited to proponents of Values Clarification. Values Clarification is merely the formal expression of an ideology which has been assimilated throughout education. Year after year I hear university students repeat, with great conviction, that "values are personal and subjective." Many of these students have never been exposed to the literature on Values Clarification. What they have been exposed to, however, is an educational culture which has rebelled against the moralizing instinct of a not-to-distant past. They are vehemently opposed to any form of "moralizing" and "preaching."

The social sciences have gone through a similar process. According to Alvin Gouldner (1962), value-freedom and neutrality provided greater autonomy for the social sciences, enhanced "a freedom from moral compulsiveness" and "encouraged at least a temporary suspension of the moralizing reflexes built into the sociologist by his own society" (p. 203). Ironically, the social sciences did not adopt the doctrine of neutrality to abstain from all value judgments. The aim, says Gouldner (1962) was to establish "a breathing space within which moral reactions could be less mechanical and in which morality could be reinvigorated. The doctrine thus had paradoxical potentiality: it might enable men to make *better* value judgments rather than *none*" (pp. 203-204).

Promoting the idea that values are personal and subjective has helped sexuality education move beyond "the tyranny of the ought." It has provided a way of addressing values in a society that is becoming increasingly pluralistic. The problem with this idea, however, is that it incorrectly equates subjectivity with subjectivism. In our effort to resist the tyranny of the ought "we have swung," as Palmer (1983) writes, to an equally tyrannical subjectivism" (p. 66). While "objectivism tells the world what it is rather than listening to what it says about itself, subjectivism is the decision to listen no one except ourselves" (p. 67).

A pedagogy that merely clarifies those values "already there" does not encourage an atmosphere of mutual accountability. It "not only neutralizes other selves; it has the same effect on the subjects we study" (p. 55).

> If the criteria of truth are my perceptions and my needs, what claims can the study of science or history or literature make on my life? This way of teaching and learning is simply one more strategy for avoiding transformation. If private knowledge (no matter how full and rich) is the measure of all things, I can never be drawn into encounter with realities outside myself - especially those that might chastise and correct me. When truth is merely "in here" we loose touch with truth's transcendence, with the critique of our illusions that comes from participating in a community... (p. 55)

Although North American society is presently characterized by a pluralism of value perspectives, it does not follow that these perspectives cannot be compared and critically evaluated (Kegan, 1982, p. 292; cf. Moran, 1989, p. 172). As Palmer (1983) emphasizes, conceding "diversity without calling us into dialogue... leaves us in isolation and destroys community as effectively as the objectivism it seeks to resist" (p. 66; cf. Barry, 1979, p. 264; Maguire, 1978, p. 180). "A simple affirmation of pluralism," writes David Tracy (1986), "can mask a repressive tolerance where all is allowed because nothing finally is taken seriously" (p. xi).

From an educational perspective, merely clarifying values "already there" cultivates the idea that all points of view are equally valid, and that the criteria of truth are whatever makes us feel good. It provides comfort but little opportunity for growth and transformation (Moran, 1987, pp. 154-155). A subjectivistic pedagogy confuses integrity with validity. As Kegan (1982) emphasizes, while persons have unqualified integrity, value positions have qualified validity (pp. 291-293). (This issue will be examined more fully in chapter six.)

2.4. The Issue of Neutrality

From a philosophical perspective, the commitment to value neutrality rests on the assumption that there exists an "archimedian point" outside of history where one can be free of subjectivity, bias, and prejudice (Bernstein, 1985; Jagger, 1983). It fails to recognize that as humans, unlike physical or material phenomena, we mediate our experience and understanding with meaning. We define ourselves and interpret our experience through dialogue, symbols, rituals, storytelling (Guindon, 1989). The known, in other words, is always mediated by the subjectivity, historical context, and language of the knower. According to Gadamer (1975), "the standpoint that is beyond any standpoint, a standpoint from which we could conceive its true identity, is a pure illusion" (p. 339). We enter a world that is already pre-interpreted in language. Language mediates our values, and the place outside of language does not exist (Gadamer, 1976).

The commitment to neutrality assumes that objectivity is best achieved through neutrality. But as Gadamer (1976) writes, this view rests on a "eunuch-like" concept of objectivity. Here "the understander is seen not in relationship to the hermeneutic situation and the constant operativeness of history in his own consciousness, but in such a way as to imply that his own understanding does not enter into the event" (p. 28).

In his most provocative thesis Gadamer argues that prejudice (which in German refers to prejudgment or pre-understanding) and values are what makes understanding and knowing possible. This thesis is particularly provocative for sexuality education as it focuses on the constructive, rather than the problematic, relationship between values, valuing and objectivity. Gadamer's thesis does not suggest that scientific research or classroom teaching "should" be distorted by ideology and bias. Rather values and "prejudices" are seen as constitutive of all understanding. Values are not mere tools for decision-making. They exist "prior to" understanding and "constitute our being." They "constitute the initial directedness of our whole ability to experience" (p. 9). Values and prejudices are not inevitable limitations in the pursuit of objective knowledge, but "biases of our openness to the world" (p. 9).[6]

Gadamer's thesis relates to the concept of the hermeneutical circle, and particularly Heidegger's (1962) discussion of its positive value. The hermeneutical circle refers to the relationship between the part and the whole in understanding. In this relationship, the part only makes sense in relationship to the whole and vice versa.

The image of the circle addresses a basic contention in hermeneutics that understanding is always contextual. The classic example is to say that a word can only be understood in relationship to the sentence, a sentence in relationship to the paragraph and so on. In turn, the paragraph can only be understood in relationship to the particular sentences within the paragraph, and sentences only in relationship to the words. The circle refers to the dialectical relationship between the whole and the part. Anthropologist Clifford Geertz (1983) describes this relationship well in saying that it involves "a continuous dialectical tacking between the most local of local detail and the most global of global structure in such a way as to bring them into simultaneous view" (p. 69).

The hermeneutical circle refers to the ontological dimension of understanding. Understanding is always preceded (not methodologically but ontologically) by a pre-understanding. The circle is not a technique for understanding, but "the expression of the existential fore-structure of Dasein (being) itself" (Heidegger, 1962, p. 185).

Hence, for Heidegger and Gadamer, there can never be a presuppositionless interpretation. Interpretation is always grounded on a type of "fore-sight" or "fore-conception" which is constitutive of our being in the world. If the hermeneutical circle is seen as a vicious circle, "as an inevitable imperfection, then the act of understanding has been misunderstood from the ground up" (Heidegger, 1962, p. 194). The circle is not an unfortunate limitation, something to be "merely tolerated." Rather, it is a productive "possibility of the most primordial kind of knowing." The main issue is "not to get out of the circle but to come into it the right way" (p. 195). Values, in other words, are not inevitable imperfections or the curse of subjectivity, but the very conditions which make meaningful knowledge and understanding possible.

This view of the relationship between knowledge and values is supported by recent developments in the history and philosophy of science. This work was spearheaded by Thomas Kuhn (1970) who outlined how scientific theories are based on traditions of research which condition the selection of research topics and interpretation of data. More recently, Mary Hesse (1980) has argued that data in both natural and social sciences are "not detachable from theory, for what count as data are determined in light of some theoretical interpretation, and the facts themselves have to be reconstructed in light of interpretation" (p. 171). According to Hesse, all science, whether natural or social, "is irreducibly metaphorical and inexact. . ." (p. 172; cf. Keller, 1985).

In modern physics there is a growing conviction that the physicist, in addition to observing the properties of atomic phenomena, also participates in their creation. Rejecting the "sharp Cartesian division between mind and matter, between the observer and the observed," physicists are asserting that "we can never speak about nature without, at the same time, speaking about ourselves... The patterns scientists observe in nature are intimately connected with the patterns of their mind; with their concepts, thoughts, and values" (Capra, 1983, pp. 86-87; cf. Bruner, 1986, p. 130; Polanyi, 1958; Zukav, 1979).

This understanding of knowledge, values, and objectivity implies that teachers should consciously seek out their subjectivity, rather than hide behind the veil of neutrality. Objective teachers are those who attempt to clarify how their values shape their teaching (cf. Peshkin, 1988). As Gadamer argues, subjectivity is not an inevitable limitation in the pursuit of objectivity, but a condition that makes objectivity possible. The paradox of knowing and understanding is that the "more authentically subjective one becomes, the more genuinely objective one is" (Conn, 1986, p. 90). As Zullo and Whitehead (1983) write:

> There is no stepping out of our social contexts and religious values; no presurgical scrub that cleanses us of our own convictions and commitments. Whether we begin in the clinic or the confessional, our environs shape our visions. This is not the curse of subjectivity, but a description of the human condition. The challenge... is not cool objectivity, but a clarity and honesty about where we begin. (p. 24)

NOTES:

1. According to a study sponsored by the Alan Guttmacher Institute, the Netherlands has the lowest rate of teenage pregnancies among industrialized countries (Jones, et al., 1986). This finding is particularly interesting in that the Netherlands is a country with very little formal sexuality education. Contraceptives, however, are readily available and contraceptive education is provided by private family planning organizations as well as by the mass

media. This situation highlights the importance of seeing sexuality education as a shared responsibility.

2. In *The Sexual Creators* André Guindon (1986) challenges the use of divorce rates to argue the "case for a crisis of conjugal fidelity." The argument, says Guindon, contains "a statistical delusion." He notes that around the year 1900 the life expectancy of "the average citizen of the world was probably somewhere around thirty years." The average marriage lasted around ten years. By 1968, this expectancy grew to fifty-three years. "If there is anything new, it is that marriages today hold firm for a much longer span of time than they ever did in human history" (p. 102).

3. Another legitimate concern is whether values clarification techniques are sophisticated enough to do what they were designed to do, that is, clarify values. Value ranking, for example, is one of the more popular value clarification strategies. The exercise asks students to rank their values or value choices in order of importance. Ranking is seen as a way of drawing out those values that are considered most important. It is said to best reveal the hierarchical structure of value thinking (Samson, 1987). Although value ranking exercises may help to raise important issues, they rest on the assumption "that values must be chosen at the expense of others" (Robb, 1985, p. 215). They also present a limited number of viable alternatives, and leave little room for contextual considerations. Other exercises, such as values voting, leave students the impression that sexual problems or issues require social consensus rather than moral scrutiny (Samson, 1979). For Boyd and Bogden (1984) Values Clarification is "not an educational methodology to help children with 'the problem of deciding what is good and what is right and what is desirable;' rather it is a collection of strategies to ensure that children arrive at 'something' that is produced by the VC strategies" (p. 290).

4. This may explain why the most common euphemisms of young people for sexual relations are "doing it" and "making out."

5. "Postponing sexual involvement" is the name of a popular program that was recently developed in Atlanta (Howard, 1983, 1985, 1990). The most striking feature of this program is its title. If persons are sexual beings from at least birth, how can young persons postpone their sexual involvement? This makes little sense unless "sexual involvement" is another euphemism for coitus.

6. In response to criticism that Gadamer's philosophy may be too conservative, Richard Bernstein (1985) argues that there is a radical and even "subversive quality" in Gadamer's writings. To support this claim Bernstein refers to Gadamer's constant critique of fanaticism and dogmatism and to an essay published by Gadamer in 1934 which was intended as a political

statement against the emerging Nazism of that period. As Bernstein writes, this was "a politically subversive and courageous act" (p. 253).

CHAPTER 3

Sexuality Education and Lawrence Kohlberg's Theory of Moral Development

Lawrence Kohlberg's theory of cognitive moral development has evolved over a period of 30 years. The sheer amount of empirical research, doctoral dissertations, philosophical reflection, and controversy generated by the theory is testimony to Kohlberg's enormous impact in this area (see Kohlberg, Levine & Hewer, 1983; Kuhmerker, Gielen, & Hayes, 1991; Modgil & Modgil, 1986; Schrader, 1990). Kohlberg has placed moral development research and moral values education on the map of academic disciplines.

The aim of this chapter is to evaluate Kohlberg's contribution to sexuality education. Does the theory represent a significant advance on Values Clarification? Are its philosophical foundations adequate for sexuality education? The chapter examines: (1) the parameters of Kohlberg's theory; (2) his philosophy of moral education; (3) his views on sexuality education; and (4) Carol Gilligan's critique of Kohlberg's formalism.

3.1. Kohlberg's Theory of Cognitive-Moral Development

Kohlberg's theory is an attempt to expand Jean Piaget's (1948) research on the moral thinking of children. Based on his observation of children as they played street games, Piaget identified "two moralities" "which follow from one another without however constituting definite stages" (p. 193). The first is "a morality of constraint or heteronomy" and the second is "a morality of cooperation or of autonomy" (p. 195).

Kohlberg's basic thesis (1980, 1981, 1984) is that moral judgment does, as Piaget had suggested, go through a developmental sequence, from heteronomy to increasing autonomy. For Kohlberg this developmental sequence involves definite stages. He expands Piaget's "two moralities" (pre-moral and moral) into four stages (two preconventional and two conventional) and adds two post-conventional stages.

Moral stages, Kohlberg (1981) affirms, follow the same structural pattern as Piaget's "two moralities." The stages are "structured wholes" in that individuals at any given stage will be consistent in their judgments. They involve "total ways of thinking." They also form an "invariant sequence" in development since stage sequence is always forwards and never backwards (except in conditions of extreme trauma). The stages are "hierarchical integrations," that is, lower stage thinking is integrated into the next stage (pp. 136-147).

Evidence of a developmental sequence in moral judgment was obtained through longitudinal and cross-cultural studies which asked people to respond to three hypothetical moral dilemmas. The Heinz dilemma was the most widely used of the three. In this dilemma Heinz must choose between two conflicting moral claims (the legal right of the druggist versus the right to life of Heinz's wife). The interviewee is then asked what Heinz should do and why he should do it. The justification of the reply establishes the structure and general patterns of moral thinking. Kohlberg expressed this pattern as six universal stages of cognitive-moral development, which move from preconventional through conventional and to postconventional levels (see Kohlberg, 1980, pp. 15-98). He concluded that "the nature of our sequence is not significantly affected by widely varying social, cultural, or religious conditions. The only thing affected is the rate at which individuals progress through this sequence" (p. 25).

For Kohlberg moral growth is basically a movement toward greater autonomy. "Moral autonomy is King" (1980, p. 71). A morally mature person is someone able to make autonomous judgments based on the principle of universal justice.

Moral development can also be described as the growth of an internal moral logic. Each new stage, each advancement in moral logic, is the result of "the combined criteria of differentiation and integration" (1981, p. 147). This dual process, according to Kohlberg, "entails a better equilibrium" of cognitive moral structures. The structure becomes more "comprehensive, differentiated, and equilibrated" in each stage (p. 147). It reaches its most equilibrated form in stage 6; the ideal and goal of moral development. Kohlberg summarizes this process in the following passage.

> When one's concept of human life moves from stage 1 to stage 2, the value of life becomes more differentiated from the value of property, more integrated (the value of life enters an organizational hierarchy where it is "higher" than property so that one steals property in order to save life), and more universalized (the life of any sentient being is valuable regardless of status or property). (p. 26)

Each new stage represents a more adequate way of dealing with moral problems since each new stage represents a more equilibrated understanding of justice. "Justice is central to the cognitive-structural transformation involved in movement from stage to stage..." Hence, Kohlberg affirms that higher stages are morally better (pp. 101-189).

For Kohlberg, morality consists primarily of competing claims ("you versus me"), rights, duties and obligations. The criteria for resolving competing claims are formal: universalization, logical consistency, and impersonality. Moral judgments are grounded on objective, impersonal, or ideal grounds. In short, "the essence of morality is respect for norms, and differences in the content of these norms are irrelevant to the fact that they involve the moral form" (Kohlberg, 1980, p. 35).

Justice, understood primarily as "fairness," is the organizing principle that can best solve competing claims. Here Kohlberg appeals to John Rawls' (1971) theory of justice. In Rawls' theory we must imagine ourselves in the "original position" under the "veil of ignorance." We are not aware of our race, sex, socio-economic status, history or future. We are, however, self-interested. If called to pass a law, we will presumably select a just law, one that can be universalized to all those concerned, or all those possibly concerned. In other words, given the uncertainty of our own status, where we could conceivably become a victim of that law, we will make sure that the law is fair for everyone.

3.2. Kohlberg's Philosophy of Moral Values Education

For Kohlberg (1981) the aim of moral values education is development. The role of educators is to stimulate development toward higher stages, where one's thinking is more just and more autonomous (pp. 49-96). This approach offers a way beyond the extremes of indoctrination and value relativity. One does not inculcate an arbitrary content or "bag of virtues." Nor does one promote a "laissez-faire" pedagogy. Instead, one stimulates the growth of a natural developmental process which evolves through successive stages of moral thinking. "The approach is non-indoctrinative," argues Kohlberg (1974):

> because it aims to stimulate the student to take the next step in his own development through a natural sequence. It rests on the natural tendency of the student to prefer the highest stage which he can comprehend - a preference which has been shown to hold regardless of the prestige or authority of the teacher or counselor. (p. 115)

Kohlberg's philosophy of education is rooted in the developmental tradition in psychology (Piaget, 1948, 1976) and the progressive movement in education (Dewey, 1956, 1959, 1963). Progressivism, says Kohlberg (1981), is one of three "streams in the development of Western educational ideology" (p. 51). The other two streams are the "Romantic" and "Cultural Transmission" ideologies. He rejects their underlying: 1) psychological theories, 2) epistemological assumptions and 3) value positions. According to Kohlberg, the Romantic model: 1) is limited by its metaphor of organic growth; 2) its epistemology places too exclusive an emphasis on self and inner experience; 3) mistakenly correlates freedom and value relativity. On the other hand, the cultural transmission model: 1) erroneously understands development "through the metaphor of the machine;" 2) its epistemology places too much emphasis on environment and object; 3) it transmits a particular set of societal values (pp. 51-73). In contrast, the progressive model: 1) sees development as an interactive process; 2) its epistemology integrates subject and object; and 3) "rejects traditional standards and value relativism in favor of ethical universals" (p. 73).

Kohlberg espouses Piaget's (1948) view of teacher as a "collaborator and not a master" (p. 412). Moral education must not take place in "an atmosphere of authority and intellectual and moral constraints" (p. 412). Educators should consider children's "lived experience" and respect their "freedom of investigation, outside of which any acquisition of human values is only an illusion" (Piaget, 1976, pp. 125-126).

Piaget, like John Dewey, advocated an interactive pedagogy. To this end, he saw advantages in pedagogical models of "self-government" (pp.118-26). Piaget's vision of the school was one where "individual experimentation and reflection carried out in common come to each other's aid" (1948, p. 412). He rejected educational systems which are too hermetic, as well as those which absolutize individual freedom (cf. Dewey, 1956, 1963).

For Kohlberg (1981), therefore, genuine education is liberal and democratic. "The notion of educational democracy," says Kohlberg, "is one in which justice between teacher and child means joining in a community in which value decisions are made on a shared and equitable basis, rather than noninterference with the child's value decisions" (p. 75). In his later work Kohlberg was especially interested in the development of just community schools in the Boston area (Schrader, 1990).

3.3. Sexuality Education and Sexual Moral Development

In the early 1970s, Kohlberg presented a paper to the Sex Information and Education Council of the United States (SIECUS) where he outlined the implications of moral development theory for sexuality education. In this paper Kohlberg criticized the purely "scientific" approach which only attempts to transmit information. Although recognizing the importance of teaching facts in sexuality education, Kohlberg (1974) argued that "facts in themselves and greater knowledge of the facts, will not resolve moral decisions in a satisfactory way without more adequate principles of moral judgment" (p. 119). He suggested that sexuality education should "encourage an analytic consideration of the factual consequences of decisions and the need for the individual student to generate his own positions and his own reasons for it" (p. 119).

Kohlberg (1971) also criticized the new interest in values clarification for its inability to go beyond the mere clarification of one's values. He rejected the idea that values clarification, by itself, would promote responsible decision making. "To promote mature decision processes," sexuality education "must attempt to stimulate the development of underlying principles" (p. 15).

The plea for a more principled approach to sexuality education was reinforced by research on sexual-moral development which found that moral reasoning about sexual dilemmas follows the same structural pattern as stages in general moral reasoning.

> In spite of discrepancies between the general level of moral reasoning and the level of reasoning about sex... thinking about sex can be conceptualized from a structural developmental point of view where the level of moral reasoning attained influences attitudes and possibly behaviors. (Gilligan, Kohlberg, Lerner, & Belenky 1971, p. 150)

Gilligan (1974) found that "different stages of moral development describe different ways of thinking about sexual relationships and different philosophies as to the place of sex in human life" (p. 102). Based on a study of high school students who were asked to respond to moral dilemmas about premarital sex, sexual rights in marriage, and teen-age pregnancy, Gilligan described a movement through four stages. These stages correspond to stages two to five in Kohlberg's theory.

In the first stage, the orientation is primarily hedonistic. The person in this stage "has no notion of a relational responsibility generated by engaging in sexual acts," and does not "invoke standards or generalized expectations shared with the partner, with the family, with the group or with society." The second stage "is characterized by a concern with shared role expectations for sexual behavior - that is, toward being a good person of whom others would approve or a loving person for whom sex is an expression of love." "Right and wrong serve to uphold group standards and maintaining group approval" (pp. 103-104). In the third stage the person is concerned with responsibility. To be responsible in sexual relationships means "being in the position to accept the consequences of one's actions" (pp. 104-105). In stage five the orientation is primarily toward mutuality. Responsibility is derived "from agreements between the two people in deciding the rightness and wrongness of sex." According to Gilligan, "this can be characterized as the civil rights attitude toward sex" (p. 105).

In spite of similarities between general moral reasoning and reasoning about sexual dilemmas, Gilligan did find important discrepancies. Subjects who reasoned according to stage 4 arguments in non-sexual issues tended to use reasoning that reflected a stage 2 orientation in sexual issues. Hence, she noted what appeared to be a relativistic regression (from stage 4 to 2) when moving from non-sexual to sexual issues. She emphasized, however, that this reasoning could not be clearly labeled as stage 2. It appeared much more as a developmental transition where young people, searching for their place in society, begin to question the validity of conventional moral standards.

In another study Jean-Marc Samson (1978) did not find the same discrepancy between the level of general moral judgment and sexual moral judgment in adolescence. He did, however, find many "regressions" from stage 4 to 3.

In yet another study, Marchand-Jodoin and Samson (1982) interviewed subjects who advanced in their level of general moral judgment but "regressed" in their level of sexual moral judgment. The researchers concluded that "it is extremely difficult to accede to stage 5 where sexual questions are concerned" (p. 255). The subjects interviewed rarely placed sexual-moral dilemmas in the perspective of postconventional morality. They "sought out another type of moral argumentation" (p. 255).

According to Samson (1979), accession to stage 6 is especially difficult since the general characteristics of a stage 6 philosophy of sexuality have not yet been outlined. Given that contemporary philosophy is just beginning to come to grips with the issues and questions of the sexual revolution, "it is not surprising that there are difficulties in developing a sexual morality at the postconventional level" (p. 261). This demands "that the individual becomes an innovative philosopher, and that is not the appanage of everyone" (p. 255).

While it is true, as Samson suggests, that modern philosophy has written little on sexuality, the question that remains unexplored is whether Kohlberg's theory represents an adequate foundation for a philosophy of sexuality. Could the discrepancies found in the research indicate a problem with the theory itself? Could the search "for another type of moral argumentation" reveal a problem with Kohlberg's formalism?

The following dilemma, which Kohlberg (1974) used as an example of how the developmental approach could be used in sexuality education, is particularly revealing.

> A boy and girl fall in love in high school and get married right after
> graduation. They never had sexual relations before marriage. After
> they are married the girl finds that she doesn't like having sexual
> intercourse with her husband. Reluctantly her husband persuades
> her to go to a marriage counselor and she asks the marriage
> counselor: "do I have an obligation to sleep with him?" (p. 120)

Furthermore:

> The wife says she wants to stay married and the husband says the
> same thing, but he goes on to say: "I met another girl and I want to
> have sexual relations with her, I asked my wife if she minded since
> she wouldn't sleep with me, if I slept with somebody else and she
> said, no, it wouldn't bother her. Is it all right for me to sleep with
> this other girl or would it be wrong to?" (p. 120)

The problem with this dilemma is that it applies the legalistic
language of a Heinz dilemma - involving duty, obligation and
competing claims - to an area of moral life that is best explored through
relational language. Constructed from an ethic of rights it obscures those
attitudes and values that relate more specifically to human sexuality, for
example, love, care, tenderness, commitment and responsibility. The
dilemma, in other words, is based on a philosophy that reduces sexual
morality entirely to issues of justice and rights. The result is a moral
problem that is somewhat awkward and unrealistic.

As ethicist André Guindon indicates, the reduction of morality to
justice:

> goes against a long and uninterrupted tradition of moral philosophy
> which considered that justice is not the only moral value. As soon
> as one realizes that the reduction of morality to justice is one of
> Kohlberg's main philosophical assumptions, it becomes obvious
> that the meaning of his sequence of stages loses much of its validity
> for a *comprehensive* understanding of moral development, and
> specifically, for sexual ethics and education. (personal
> communication, October 26, 1985)

3.4. Toward a More Relational Ethic

The most penetrating critique of Kohlberg has come from his colleague Carol Gilligan (1977, 1980, 1982, 1988a, 1988b). Gilligan's critique was sparked by the suspicion of a male bias in the scoring protocols. Women were either excluded entirely from research samples or classified lower than men (particularly at stage 3) in stages of cognitive moral development.

In a now famous study on abortion Gilligan (1977) interviewed women who spoke a moral language embedded with relational imagery. The women in this study saw morality through categories such as care, love and responsibility. Due to this relational "bias," women were scored at lower stages. Here lies the paradox, says Gilligan (1977):

> for the very traits that have traditionally defined the "goodness" of women, their care for and sensitivity to the needs of others, are those that mark them as deficient in moral development. The infusion of feeling into their judgments keeps them from developing a more independent and abstract ethical conception in which concern for others derives from principles of justice rather than from compassion and care. (p. 484)

The women in Gilligan's study went through roughly three moral phases. At the first level the orientation was primarily to individual survival. The movement to the second level was characterized by a transition from selfishness to responsibility. Here the women were struggling with the concept of responsibility and trying to balance the tension between compassion and autonomy, virtue and power. In the next transition, responsibility was understood in terms of self and other. According to Gilligan, this marked a transition from goodness to truth, from an act-centered to a life-centered morality. In the final stage, which is also described as postconventional, the women asserted the moral equality between self and other. The principle of non-violence, an "ethic of care," and responsibility to self and other were now central to moral life (Gilligan, 1982, pp. 100-105).

The findings of this study led Gilligan to challenge the ethical and developmental assumptions of Kohlberg's theory. The women's "voice" she claims, is not deficient, only different. It reflects a "different social and moral understanding" (Gilligan, 1977, p. 482). For Gilligan (1988a), Kohlberg is guilty of "moral reductionism, the temptation to simplify human dilemmas by claiming that there is only one moral standpoint" (p xxvii).

Gilligan argues that moral development theory must integrate the voice of relationality if it is to build a holistic vision of moral maturity. It must integrate justice and care, rationality and relationality, autonomy and attachment (Gilligan, 1980). A theory based on justice and autonomy alone offers a truncated vision of moral maturity. It points to a conception of adulthood "that is itself out of balance" (Gilligan, 1982, p. 17).

In her most recent work Gilligan (1988a) attempts to redefine moral maturity as the "ability to see in at least two ways and to speak at least two languages . . . " (p. xx). She is particularly critical of developmental models which equate "adulthood with a justice perspective, and maturity with separation, self-sufficiency, and independence" (p. v). Kohlberg's theory reflects the dominant ideology of contemporary psychology which understands maturity and growth as the process by which "the individual is embarked on a solitary journey toward personal salvation... " (p. xxvii). Reliance on others is seen as "a sign of limitation and associated with childhood dependence, the ways in which people can and do help one another tend not to be represented" (p. xxxii). According to Gilligan, maturity as self-sufficiency or independence "presumes a radical discontinuity of generation and encourages a view of human experience that is essentially divorced from history or time" (p. xxii). It reflects a masculinist ideology which equates "human with male" (Gilligan, 1988b, p. 18).

A more balanced view of human and moral development would rest on a different conception of self. It would see reliance on others as "part of the human condition" and would recognize that people do "rely on one another for understanding, comfort, and love." In a more relational ethic "the values of care and connection, salient in women's thinking, imply a view of self and other as interdependent and of relationships as networks created and sustained by attention and response" (p. 8). In a care perspective,

> being dependent, then, no longer means being helpless, powerless, and without control; rather, it signifies a conviction that one is able to have an effect on others, as well as the recognition that the interdependence of attachment empowers both the self and the other, not one person at the other's expense. (p. 16)

Gilligan brings an important corrective to Kohlberg's theory. Her vision of moral development draws attention to the ecological perspective discussed in the previous chapter. According to Moran (1983a), Gilligan's ethic of care and responsibility, and her understanding of moral maturity as "principled non-violence," reintroduces the idea of prudence in moral language. Prudence, which Moran defines as "careful knowing," is not a matter of decision-making alone but of *listening* "to the rhythms of the body and of nature . . ." (p. 100).

Although Gilligan is not speaking from a religious or theological perspective, an ethic based on care and responsibility also reintroduces the religious idea of gift into moral language. When morality is seen as an "autonomous institution," as Hauerwas (1980) writes, "the idea that life is a gift can only appear heteronomous. For it is assumed that autonomy entails the attempt to free myself from all relations except those I freely choose and the language of gift continues only to encourage dependence" (p. 444; cf. Moran, 1989).

Drawing heavily on Niebuhr's (1963) notion of responsibility, Gilligan no longer defines the human as a "strong man" who stands isolated from others and who "owes his strength to being alone" (Arendt, 1958, p. 188). The eco-logic ethic proposed by Gilligan challenges the major assumptions of *homo faber*. In an ethic of responsibility, the human is not primarily a "maker" but an "answerer." The moral self is an agent in relation and morality is placed in "a context of human interaction" (Gilligan, 1980, p. 235). An ethic of response insists on a contextual understanding of morality and "restores the narrative to moral discussion, locating accountability in the interchange of interpretation and response, placing moral inquiry in a context of historical time and place, and tying responsibility to the social solidarity of ongoing community" (p. 234).

In his response to Gilligan, Kohlberg argues that an ethic of responsibility refers to a different type of decision-making, namely decision-making in the realm "of kinship, love, friendship, and sex" (Kohlberg, Levine, & Hewer, 1983, p. 22). An ethic of responsibility is seen as particularly appropriate for personal issues involving "relations of special obligations to family and friends" (p. 22). The imagery and language discussed above, however, suggests an even more radical critique. It calls into question the very idea of formal decision-making as the central metaphor of moral life. For Gilligan moral growth is not characterized by the growth of an internal moral logic or self-reliant "decision-making," but rather as a process of interpretation, dialogue and responsiveness to human need (cf. Hauerwas, 1980, pp 476-477; Gadamer, 1975, p. 288).

In restoring the narrative to moral reflection Gilligan's work highlights the importance of contextuality and meaning. It would be a mistake, however, to see contextuality and universality as opposite poles. This would lead to a misplaced debate with Gilligan's contextual ethic on one side and Kohlberg's principled ethic on the other.

As far back as Aristotle, philosophers have described ethical reflection as a dialectical tension between general norms or principles and their application in concrete circumstances. Aristotle saw ethical reflection as a matter of interpretation, that is, a process of discerning the meaning of a norm within a particular context. A norm, in other words, only makes sense when it is applied (Gadamer, 1975; cf. Maguire, 1978).

Furthermore, there is a problem with Gilligan's understanding of the source of justice and care. Although Gilligan is careful not to suggest that an ethic of care characterizes exclusively the morality of women and justice the morality of men, she does identify care with relationship and connection, while justice is identified with autonomy and separation (Gilligan, 1980). In merely adding "to Kohlberg's focus on justice a complementary ethic of care" (p. 248), there is a danger of perpetuating a dichotomous view of moral development, a view that would impoverish our understanding of both justice and care. As Gabriel Moran (1987), indicates, "justice arises out of care, the attentiveness to the needs of each bodily thing. To speak of a complementary of justice and care is to imply that justice is care-less or unfeeling" (p. 82; cf. Maguire, 1978, pp. 94-99).

In response to this criticism Gilligan (1988a) insists that "these two approaches are not opposites or mirror images of one another (with justice uncaring and care unjust). Instead they constitute different ways of organizing the problem that lead to different reasoning strategies, different ways of thinking about what is happening and what to do" (p. xxi; cf. Vreeke, 1991). The problem remains, however, that a dichotomous view of justice and care fails to appreciate how the two ethics overlap. As Marilyn Friedman (1987) writes, Gilligan fails to acknowledge

> the potential for *violence and harm* in human interrelationships and
> human community. The concept of justice, in general, arises out of

relational conditions in which most human beings have the capacity, and many have the inclination, to treat each other badly... The complex reality of social life encompasses the human potential for helping, caring for, and nurturing others *as well as* the potential for harming, exploiting, and oppressing others. Thus, Gilligan is wrong to think that the justice perspective completely neglects 'the reality of human relationships.' Rather it arises from a more complex, and more realistic, estimate of the nature of human interrelationship. (pp. 104-105; cf. Conn, 1986, p. 98; Guindon, 1991, p. 3; Nielson, 1987b, p. 396)

Kohlberg, therefore, does provide an important step beyond the subjectivism of Values Clarification. His reduction of morality to formal decision-making and to competing claims, however, provides an inadequate basis for a theory of values in sexuality education. Although Gilligan does not account for the interrelationship between justice and care, her critique of Kohlberg points to the importance of restoring the narrative to moral reflection. (This issue will be examined more fully in chapter six.)

PART TWO

TOWARDS A MORE HOLISTIC VIEW
OF SEXUAL-VALUES EDUCATION

CHAPTER 4

Robert Kegan's Theory of Human Development

Robert Kegan's theory of human development provides a way in which to go beyond the Kohlberg-Gilligan debate, and beyond the overly reductionistic and instrumental view of values and sexuality education discussed in chapter two. In the Prologue to *The Evolving Self* Kegan (1982) writes that his foundational question is metaphysical. "Psychology asks fundamental questions about being human" (p. 2). It attends to the "zone of mediation where meaning is made." At its best, it tries to understand the experience of a person "in the way he or she experiences it," in the meanings he or she gives to that experience (p. VIII).

Kegan's theory provides a holistic perspective on human development. Here the term "holistic" refers "to an understanding of reality in terms of integrated wholes whose properties cannot be reduced to those of smaller units" (Capra, 1983, p. 38). In contrast, a reductionistic view of reality is animated by "the belief that all aspects of a complex phenomenon can be understood by reducing them to their constituent parts" (p. 59).

Capra's distinction between a narrow and broader meaning of holism helps to clarify *how* Kegan's theory is holistic. In a "narrow" understanding of holism "the human organism is seen as a living system whose components are all interconnected and interdependent." A "broader" view "recognizes also that this system is an integral part of larger systems, which implies that the individual organism is in continual interaction with its physical and social environment, that it is constantly affected by the environment but can also act upon it and modify it" (p. 317, see also: pp. 265-304).

Kegan's theory is holistic in both senses. It refuses to reduce "human" or "development" to only one category. It examines the relationship between the organism and the environment, self and other, subject and object, cognition and emotion, the individual and the social, as well as the relationship between the past, present, and future. It is holistic in the "broader" view in that it not only acknowledges the existences of these parts, but more significantly, it examines how the parts are interconnected and constructed in an integrated system. In this integrated system, development is characterized by its relations rather than its parts. It is dynamic and involves process rather than mere structure or stages, and is cyclical rather than exclusively hierarchical or linear.

Kegan's holistic perspective is the fruit of an interdisciplinary dialogue. The theory is grounded in empirical research, informed by philosophy, theology and the world of literature and was developed through a conceptual dialogue between the constructive-developmental, the psychoanalytic and the phenomenological-existential traditions in psychology (Kegan, 1970, 1977, 1980).

The nature of this dialogue can best be described as constructive and relational. According to William Rogers (1980), the strength of a "constructive-relational" approach is that it

> remains faithful to the primary phenomena, while encouraging relational attention to multiple disciplines of interpretation - moving toward a more constructive and holistic understanding (that cannot be "claimed" or reduced by any of the various approaches). Here there may be both mutual critique and support, empirical attentiveness, and innovative possibilities for integration. (pp. 16-17; cf. Baum, 1981)

Kegan, who describes himself as a "teacher, therapist, and researcher-theorist" (1982, p. viii), teaches at the Harvard Graduate School of Education. His doctoral dissertation was on Jean Piaget. He has worked closely with Lawrence Kohlberg, Carol Gilligan, William Perry, James Fowler and others associated with the Harvard Graduate School of Education and the Harvard Center for Moral Education. He and his research associates at Harvard have developed a research interview based on the theory discussed in this book. Although he may not be as well known as some of his Harvard colleagues, his work has had considerable influence on the work of scholars interested in the study of human and moral development from both a psychological and philosophical perspective (see especially Conn, 1986; Guindon, 1989a, 1990, 1992).

This chapter delineates the major components of Kegan's theory. It examines: 1) the Piagetian roots of Kegan's epistemology; 2) the influence of Erik Erikson; 3) Kegan's conceptualization of meaning-making as foundational to human development; 4) the dialectical tension between autonomy and attachment; 5) the values underlying Kegan's imagery of development; and 6) the role and function of the cultures of embeddedness.

4.1.   Jean Piaget and the Constructive-Developmental Approach

To fully appreciate Kegan's theory, it is important to first consider the influence of Jean Piaget and Erik Erikson. Although a complete treatment of their work is beyond the scope of this chapter, I will briefly consider those elements that are central to the development of Kegan's theory.   One of Kegan's aims is to bridge psychoanalytic and constructive-developmental theory.[1]

Kegan's theory is largely rooted in Jean Piaget's epistemology. For Piaget (1954), knowing is an interactive and constructive process. The mind actively constructs reality. Like Immanuel Kant, Piaget refuted the empiricists' claim that the mind is epistemologically passive. Unlike traditional Kantianism, however, Piaget placed considerable emphasis on environment and knowing, particularly on the interaction or dialectic between mind and environment. The mind actively constructs reality through interaction with the environment. It seeks to establish an equilibrium between the self and reality (pp. 355-360).

Reality is not known solely in self (subject) or other (object). Knowledge, in other words, is never purely objective or purely subjective. Reality is known precisely where subject and object (self-other) meet: "all knowledge is simultaneously accommodation to the object and assimilation to the subject, the progress of intelligence works in the dual direction of externalization and internalization" (p. 357). Intelligence is a dynamic and interactive activity and not a static thing or "quotient."

Piaget's (1970) genetic epistemology challenged social learning theory which saw the psychological structures of learning as a product of one's environment. Philosophically, it challenged those epistemologies that saw knowing either as the passive product of the environment or the innate structures of the mind (pp. 9-10). Piaget's approach is referred to as "constructive" because knowing is seen as "a process of continual construction and organization" (p. 2).

> To know is to assimilate reality into systems of transformations. To know is to transform reality... Knowing reality means constructing systems of transformations that correspond, more or less adequately, to reality... Knowing an object does not mean copying it - it means acting upon it. (p. 15)

Central to this epistemology is the notion of "decentering:" the self's cognitive desire to go beyond itself; the movement from subjectivity to objectivity (Piaget, 1954, p. 357). This movement toward objectivity is a movement beyond an overly subjective orientation and not beyond subjectivity as such. Subjectivity remains central. Through decentering, subjectivity is reappropriated in structurally and qualitatively different ways.

Piaget refers to this overly subjective orientation as "egocentrism." It is important to emphasize, however, that egocentrism, for Piaget, refers to an epistemological reality (i.e. where one's way of knowing is too subjective) and not to a moral quality. It is also important to point out that this dynamism is primarily cognitive. Affect is a motivating force developing parallel to cognition and inseparable from cognitional structures. Affect, however, has no cognitional value in itself (Piaget, 1968, pp. 33-60; Conn, 1981, pp. 60-89).

Piaget's (1948) understanding of knowing as relational and interactive is also evident in his study of moral judgment. Autonomy, for Piaget, does not involve separation from others. On the contrary, moral judgment develops through social interaction, through mutual respect, cooperation and reciprocity.

> Truthfulness is necessary to the relations of sympathy and mutual respect. Reciprocity seems in this connection to be the determining factor of autonomy... apart from our relations to other people, there can be no moral necessity. The individual as such knows only anomie and not autonomy. Conversely, any relation with other persons, in which unilateral respect takes place, leads to heteronomy. Autonomy therefore appears only with reciprocity, when mutual respect is strong enough to make the individual feel from within the desire to treat others as he himself would wish to be treated. (p. 194)

The epistemological activity of subject-object relations is translated, in the moral domain, to interpersonal relations. Moral knowing is primarily relational. It involves balancing self and other, or autonomy and reciprocity.

Although Piaget was primarily concerned with cognition, he does see an implicit relationship between cognition and affect in moral judgment. Cooperation among children requires feelings of mutual respect. In the development of both cognitive and moral judgment structures, affect is seen as a motivating force behind this process. Affect, however, is not seen as an epistemological force.

The process described above underlies Piaget's understanding of stages and stage development. The structural reorganization of this epistemological activity, says Piaget, is a developmental phenomenon. Cognitive development is characterized by the continual process of decentering. All persons go through invariant stages of epistemo-logical development, stages where subjectivity and objectivity are in dialectical tension.

Cognitive development evolves from a sensori-motor stage, to a pre-logical stage (i.e. preoperational thought), to a logical concrete stage (concrete operations), and lastly to a formal logical stage (formal operations) (see Piaget, 1968; Conn, 1981). Higher stage thinking (i.e. greater objectivity) represents a qualitative re-organization in that it structures with increasing effectiveness more complex intellectual "operations."

Piaget's thinking is usually reduced to these stages. According to Kegan (1982), however, the genius and contribution of Piaget is not so much in his delineation of cognitive stages as it is in his study of the epistemological process that underlies stage development. Kegan is especially critical of neo-Piagetian approaches that reduce Jean Piaget to "stages." "Twenty years from now - long after the passion for descriptive stages in the life course has spent itself - Piaget may `be about' stages or cognitive development only in the way that Newton `is about' gravity... "(p. 42). The interest in stages reflects the interest and passion of a particular time. For Kegan, Piaget set the stage for an even greater discovery. Cognitive stages are just one part of a larger process, namely the constructive activity of meaning-making.

4.2. Erik Erikson and the Psycho-Social Approach

The elements of Erikson's approach that are most evident in Kegan's theory, and that are particularly relevant for this chapter are: Erikson's emphasis on the psycho-social and affective dimensions of human development, his understanding of development as lifelong, and his discussion of the relationship between sexuality, intimacy and identity. (This last area will be examined more fully in the next chapter in the discussion of Kegan's "Interpersonal" and "Interindividual" phases.)

Erikson's theory focuses on the interaction between the individual and the social. In each developmental stage, individual potentialities interact with "social modalities." Each stage has a corresponding social institution that can help or hinder development.

One of Erikson's aims was to situate sexual development within a larger social and ethical context. Erikson (1963) was concerned with the "overextension of the sexual" in Freudian theory. He sought to bridge stages of psycho-sexual and psycho-social development.

> We must search for the proper place of the libido theory in the totality of human life. While we must continue to study the life cycle of individuals by delineating the possible vicissitudes of their libido, we must become sensitive to the danger of forcing living persons into the role of marionettes of a mythical Eros. (p. 64)

Erikson shifts the Freudian focus from sexuality to personality. Personality is no longer defined by sexuality. Sexuality is one expression of the total person and sexual development has more to do with the quality of human relations than with biological transformations or physiological needs alone (cf. Francoeur, 1991, pp. 73, 433).

In the oral stage, for example, Erikson writes that "the amount of trust derived from the earliest infantile experience does not seem to depend on absolute quantities of food or demonstrations of love but on the quality of maternal relationships" (p. 249). In this stage, the quality of the maternal relationship and of the social modality form "the springs of the basic sense of trust and the basic sense of mistrust which remains the ontogenetic source of both primal hope and doom throughout life" (p. 80).

In Erikson's understanding of personality development, the sexual and moral interpenetrate. This is clearest in the sixth stage (intimacy versus isolation). Mature sexuality, says Erikson, can only develop in the context of intimacy and the ethical sense of adulthood. With the establishment of a firmer identity, the person is now ready for intimacy (p. 264). Sexual and psychological intimacy, therefore, is not a matter of fusion. Mature sexuality should include trust, autonomy, and mutuality (pp. 265-268; Erikson, 1964, pp. 111-157).

For Erikson, sexual development does not end with puberty. It is a lifelong developmental process. The adult task of generativity "is an essential stage on the psychosexual as well as the psychosocial schedule" (1963, p. 267). In the last stage, the life cycle rejoins its beginnings. The growth of hope in infancy is largely dependent on the integrity of the last stage: where childhood and adulthood, the individual and the social, the sexual and the moral, all interpenetrate.

Erikson's "eight ages of man" are summarized in table 4.1 below. In each age the growing person experiences a "crises" or tension. Listed beside each "age" is the human strength or "virtue" that arises through the successful resolution of each tension (pp. 247-274). Next to the first five ages, Freud's corresponding stage of psychosexual development are indicated. The ages highlight Erikson's concern with the affective.

Table 4.1. Erikson's Eight Ages

Stage	Virtue	Freud's Stages
1. Trust vs. Mistrust	Drive & Hope	Oral Sensory
2. Autonomy vs. Shame & Doubt	Self-control & Willpower	Muscular Anal
3. Initiative vs. Guilt	Direction & Purpose	Locomotor Genital
4. Industry vs. Inferiority	Method & Competence	Latency
5. Identity vs. Role Confusion	Devotion & Fidelity	Puberty & Adolescence
6. Intimacy vs. Isolation	Affiliation & Love	
7. Generativity vs. Stagnation	Production & Care	
8. Integrity vs. Despair	Renunciation & Wisdom	

4.3. Meaning-Making as Foundational to Human Development

Kegan reconceptualizes the tensions between the cognitive and affective, as well as the individual and the social. To ask which of these has primacy is to invite a misplaced debate. The key, says Kegan, does not lie with the poles within the tensions, but with the underlying context or foundational reality that grounds these tensions.

Kegan's (1982) main thesis is that this foundational reality or "deep structure" of human development is the activity of constructing meaning, which he calls "meaning constitutive evolutionary activity." This underlying context does not make cognition or affect, the individual or the social "the master of personality" (p. VIII). Rather, it attends to the deeper and larger context of human development. The activity of constructing meaning philosophically precedes and gives rise to cognition and affect. As James Fowler (1980) writes:

> The problem we confront here is not one of how to theoretically integrate thought and feeling. Rather, the challenge is to recognize that meaning-making, as a constructive movement, is prior to and generative of both reason and emotion. We must, Kegan asserts, see meaning making as the self's total constitutive-knowing activity, an activity in which there is no thought without feeling and no feeling without thought. (p. 60)

According to Kegan (1982), it is not "thinking" or "feeling," which motivates a person's growth. Nor is it, as psychoanalytic theory suggests, the "desire to reduce unpleasurable affect" (P. 83). The motivation resides in "the greater coherence of its organization. The organism is moved to make meaning... to preserve and enhance its integrity" (p. 84).

In psychology "only the neo-psychoanalytical (including ego psychology and object relations theory) and the existential-phenomenological traditions have been particularly interested "in the person as a meaning-maker" (p. 3). The underlying structure of the constructive-developmental paradigm, argues Kegan, is also well equipped to address the person as meaning-maker. It can offer a vision of the person that is more unified, "more dialectical and less dichotomous" (p. 8).

As was seen above, Piaget's epistemology is primarily interactive. Intellectual knowing grows through interaction between self and other, subject and object, organism and environment. Moral knowing grows through the interaction between autonomy and reciprocity. Kegan argues that this process, and not particular stages, is central to the Piagetian paradigm. Fundamentally, the activity of meaning-making is what underlines the Piagetian paradigm in its biological, psychological and philosophical dimensions (p. 294).

Self-other relating goes on in a prior context, I say, and this context has a philosophical meaning (the prior ground to the subject-object relation; the dialectic which continuously resolves the subject-object dichotomy), a biological meaning (the relative or absolute state of undifferentiation, out of which emerges, through the process of adaptation, an increasingly articulated organization), a psychological meaning (the psychologically undifferentiated "culture of embeddedness" out of which the organism emerges in its self-other constructing...). (Kegan, 1980, p. 408)

In an attempt to go beyond a strictly Piagetian approach, however, Kegan argues that meaning-making is about both knowing and being. It is an activity that is simultaneously epistemological and ontological.

The Piagetian approach, viewing meaning-making from the outside, descriptively, has powerfully advanced a conception of that activity as naturally epistemological; it is about the balancing and rebalancing of subject and object, self and other. But what remains ignored from this approach is a consideration of the same activity from the inside, what Fingarette would call the "participative." From the point of view of the "self," then, what is at stake in preserving any given balance is the ultimate question of whether the "self" shall continue to *be*, a naturally ontological matter. (1982, p. 12)

According to Kegan, development and meaning-making are about self-preservation and self-transformation, decentering and recentering, surrendering and defending. Our experience of these dialectical movements is the very source of "e-motion."

Affect is essentially phenomenological, the felt experience of a motion (hence, "e-motion"). In identifying evolutionary activity as the fundamental ground of personality I am suggesting that the source of our emotions is the phenomenological experience of evolving, of defending, surrendering, and reconstructing a new center. (pp. 81-82)

4.4. The Dialectical Tension Between Autonomy and Attachment

In Kohlberg's theory, moral growth is seen as a movement toward a more adequate construction of justice. Kohlberg's concept of justice rests on a view of self as rational and autonomous. As was seen in the previous chapter, Gilligan brings an important corrective to bear by adding a complementary ethic of care based on a view of self as connected or relational. As Nielson (1987b) writes, "with different theories of self, we get different conceptions of politics and different conceptions of the moral life" (p. 386).

Kegan's theory reconceptualizes self as constituted by *both* autonomy *and* connection. The theory brings further support to the idea that justice and care must be seen as interdependent rather than merely complementary. According to Kegan, autonomy and connection or attachment are simultaneous poles in tension throughout development. Autonomy and attachment, like subjectivity and objectivity, represent different perspectives of *one* process.

Both autonomy and attachment, says Kegan (1983), are expressive of "the two greatest yearnings in human experience" (p. 107). The human is an historical and social being who experiences the need or yearning for attachment (inclusion, communion, connection, integration) and autonomy (independence, agency, individuation, differentiation, separation). Human experience is marked by periods of separation (moving out into the world) and integration (moving back inwards). Both realities are present throughout development. "Growth itself is not alone a matter of separation and repudiation, of killing off the past. This is more a matter of transition." Growth also involves "reconciliation" and "recovery" (p. 129). Each qualitative change in human development "is a response to the complexity of the world, a response in further recognition of how the world and I are yet again distinct - and thereby more related" (p. 85).

Each new developmental "era" or "truce" in the life cycle is a temporary solution or balance of this fundamental tension in life. "Each balance resolves the tension in a different way." One balance slightly "favors autonomy" while the next balance resolves the tension slightly "in the favor of inclusion" (p. 108). The "favored" balance will define the structure and content of one's valuing (i.e. what one values). Here development is not portrayed as a straight line, but as a helix or spiral (p. 109).

4.5. Imagery, Development, and Values

Theories of human development tend to portray growth as exclusively linear. Development is conceived as moving upward and hierarchically from point A to point B, in a straight line, and tending toward a particular end-point. In Kohlberg's theory, for example, one moves hierarchically through six stages. The movement is upward and never backward. Higher stages are better than lower stages and stage 6 is the ideal and goal of cognitive-moral development.

In *No Ladder To the Sky* Gabbier Moran (1987) describes how this image has dominated Western thought. "The image of a rope, a chain, a ladder, or a stairway is one of the most widespread images in human history" (p. 3). It is ever present in psychology, in western mythology, and religious literature. The image "invites us to climb upward, and in business, government, sport or war we continue climbing the ladder of success in search of the good life" (p. 3). This search is a solitary journey as the ladder has room for only one person at a time.[2]

The image of the ladder provides a picture of "life as an elevator to the roof of a high-rise building..." (p. 175). And, as Moran observes, "what they fail to say is that you get pushed off the roof when you get there" (p. 175).

According to Nelson (1988), the image of the ladder can be linked to the body-spirit dualism which has dominated western spirituality. The "up motif" originated in Hellenistic Greece, a time when "the body-spirit dualism reigned supreme." The movement up the "ladder of virtue" was perceived as a movement "from the fleshly to the spiritual, from the earthly to the heavenly" (p. 37). The image of the ladder suggests a movement *away* from the earth.

Nelson also links linear images to the genitalization of male sexuality. In a patriarchal society, it is *male* genitalia that define what it means to be sexual. This leads to what Nelson calls an "erection mentality" (p. 90), which projects upon the world values relating to size, hardness, upness, and externality at the expense of values relating to the internal, "the cyclical, the horizontal, and the soft" (p. 90, see also pp. 90-105). Here the straight line is the symbol of performance and success, of potency and of life itself" (p. 74).

> We have been taught and have learned to value phallic meanings in patriarchy: bigger is better (in bodily height, in paychecks, in the size of one's corporation or farm); hardness is superior to softness (in one's muscles, in one's facts, in one's foreign policy positions); upness is better than downness (in one's career path, in one's computer, in one's approach to life's problems). In `a man's world,' small, soft, and down pale beside big, hard, and up. (pp. 94-95)

The helix provides an alternative image. Here development is more *cyclical*. Although there is an upward movement in the helix, the movement is not through a straight line or up the steps of a ladder. The movement of life is not portrayed as *exclusively* forward moving. With the image of the helix, and with autonomy and connection in creative tension, the steps up a ladder become steps in a dance (Kegan, 1980; cf. Moran, 1987, p. 171). The image is less individualistic and more communal.

Seen as a three dimensional image, the helix addresses the *depth* of human development. The person moves deeper rather than just higher. Moving higher means transcending one's past. Moving deeper suggests a movement out into the world as well as a movement back inwards. Moving deeper also implies a recognition of one's sense of connection, for development is "a response in further recognition of how the world and I are yet again distinct - and thereby more related" (p. 85).

It is also important to note that the helix has no specific end-point. It is continuous and lifelong. This provides a more dynamic view of development and leaves Kegan's theory open to phases beyond the "Interindividual."

4.6. Development and the Cultures of Embeddedness

"Person" in Kegan's theory refers to the individual and social together. Kegan does not understand meaning-making as something we do on our own. It is "a social activity" which "depends on someone who recognizes you." "Not meaning, by definition, is utterly lonely" (p. 19).

Throughout the lifespan individuals are embedded in particular cultures, from the "mothering culture" in infancy to the "culture of mutuality" in adulthood. Kegan refers to these cultures as "psycho-social" or "holding" environments. Each environment must perform three functions: confirmation, contradiction, and continuity (pp. 118-132).

The task of *confirmation* is "holding on." It responds primarily to the need for recognition and connection. In infancy this literally means that one is being held. Later "being held" metaphorically refers to the creation of a psychological space where one's integrity is affirmed, and where one's newly discovered abilities are both recognized and celebrated. An adequate holding environment enables the person to "emerge and meet the next moments of life" (p. 124).

The task of *contradiction* is "letting go." It responds primarily to the need for separation. It acknowledges and recognizes the movement away from an old self, from the person one was to the person one is becoming. "Letting go" is what prevents "holding on" from becoming "holding onto."

The second task is called contradiction because the cultures of embeddedness must also, at the appropriate time, challenge or confront the validity of the evolving self's present epistemological construction. In the Imperial stage, for example, confirmation means acknowledging and nurturing the child's "displays of self-sufficiency, competence, and role differentiation." Contradiction means denying "the validity of only taking one's needs into account" (p. 135). (This issue will be examined more fully in chapters five and six.)

Continuity provides an environment that allows the person to reintegrate after separation. Its task is "staying put." Moving out into the world or separation is not a matter of "killing off the past." Separation is transitional. A culture of embeddedness that "stays put," provides continuity and allows for reconciliation and recovery (Kegan, 1982, pp. 129-132).

Like Erikson, Kegan places considerable emphasis on the *quality* of these psychosocial environments. The ability to make one's world cohere, to remain in balance, to differentiate and to reintegrate, will depend largely on the presence and quality of these cultures; on their ability to confirm, contradict, and stay put at the appropriate time. The following chapter examines the characteristics and functions of each culture.

NOTES:

1. Gabbier Moran (1983) has expressed doubts about the possibility of such a task. Without referring specifically to Kegan, Moran writes that: "Anyone whose distinctive approach is Piagetian cannot incorporate Eriksonian

material. And anyone who starts with an Eriksonian pattern can incorporate Piaget only in minor ways" (p. 23). Acknowledging some similarities ("both are concerned with interaction: the relation between organism and environment" and "both try to avoid the arrogant claim of knowing what the perfected human being is") (pp. 24, 26), Moran argues that the foundational imagery of both approaches are sufficiently different to allow for a "grand synthesis."

It is important to emphasize that while Kegan's theory is rooted in Piaget, it differs substantially from most Neo-Piagetian approaches. Kegan is critical of neo-Piagetian approaches that speak solely of cognitive stages. He attempts to offer a deeper "reading" of Piaget, one which discovers "a genius who exceeded himself and found more than he was looking for" (Kegan, 1982, p. 26). It is this interpretation of Piaget that will allow Kegan to *bridge* both approaches (while not necessarily offering a "grand synthesis"). Kegan suggests that this reading of Piaget uncovers a framework that can potentially generate a more holistic understanding of persons in both their health and disease, a framework which can generate "a rich fund of those basic metaphors and images by which we come to experience our experience" (p. 42).

2. For a penetrating analysis of how animals and other forms of non-human life have been excluded from the ladder see: (Robbins, 1987). Robbins examines the human and ecological costs of so-called "progress" in the world of "modern" agribusiness. He unveils a world characterized by incredible brutality to animals, an industry that has become a major health hazard for humans, and that is posing a major threat to the planet's ecosystem. Robbins' book supports Gabbier Moran's (1987) conviction that we need a "language with which to think about the whole world of living things in a moral way" (p. 38).

CHAPTER 5

Sexuality, Valuing, and the Cultures of Embeddedness in Kegan's Developmental Stages

This chapter outlines Kegan's developmental stages: the Incorporative, Impulsive, Imperial, Interpersonal, Institutional, and Interindividual. The chapter examines the sexual and moral themes of each stage, as well as the role of the cultures of embeddedness in the transitions from stage to stage. Considerable emphasis is placed on the "cultures of embeddedness" since it is that part of Kegan's theory which has the richest educational meanings and implications. (An outline of each stage is provided in table 5.1 at the end of the chapter.)

5.1. Infancy and Early Childhood: The Incorporative and Impulsive Stages

Kegan's first stage is called *Incorporative*. The culture of embeddedness in this stage is the "mothering culture." Its task is literally to "hold" the infant. The presence of a qualitative holding environment is necessary for the child's psychological, moral, and physical development.

In the early part of this century, medicine placed considerable emphasis on making the physical environment of infants clean and antiseptic. This contributed to a popular bias (which in some cases still persists today) against holding and touching babies. The established medical wisdom advised parents and health care workers to hold infants as little as possible. Holding and touching, it was believed, would spoil the child and make him or her dependent (Colton, 1983).

According to Kegan (1982), being held is not an impediment to autonomy. On the contrary, being held is basic to the development of autonomy. It empowers the child to move out into the world. The problem is not with *holding*, but with *holding onto* (or overprotecting) at a time when the child begins to display independence.

Montagu (1971) has shown that infants will not survive the absence of a qualitative holding environment even if they are properly clothed and fed. In the 19th century it was common for infants in their first year to die of a disease called Marasmus, literally, "wasting away." Marasmus nourished itself on the absence of holding and touching (cf. Ackerman, 1991; Cohen, 1986). Prescott (1975, 1989) has shown that children who are exposed to tender and pleasurable touch in infancy are much less prone to interpersonal violence in adulthood (cf. Francoeur, 1991, pp. xix-xxi).

The Impulsive stage is the age of symbol, fantasy and imagination. Here the "child's life is filled with fantasy and fantasy about the fantastic" (Kegan, 1982, p. 136). As Pearce (1985) writes, analogy and symbolism "is the center that holds things together" (p. 60). The first role of the culture of embeddedness during this stage (the "parenting culture"), therefore, is to acknowledge and nurture the child's life of fantasy (Kegan, 1982, p. 135). Logical and factual explanations of how the world works are inadequate. "Answers to the *Why?* questions must be symbolic, metaphoric, or analogical" (Pearce, 1985, p. 60).

This stage is called "Impulsive" because children embedded in this stage have difficulty controlling their impulses. They are unable to mediate their impulses. The impulses "are the self." "When I am subject to my impulses, their non-expression raises an ultimate threat; they risk who I am" (Kegan, 1982, p. 88).

In terms of sexual development, the "Incorporative phase" includes what Freud described as the shift from orality to anality. The "Impulsive phase" sees the emergence of the oedipal period. The Impulsive child's identification with the parent of the opposite sex, however, is not simply the result of a sexual attraction. It may be, suggests Kegan, that the child simply "finds one parent the more likely vehicle by which to satisfy her many impulses" (p. 141).

Guindon compares the ethical perspective of this stage with "hedonism" (1989a, pp. 51-56; 1992, pp. 48-52). The moral imperative of hedonism is to seek pleasure and avoid pain. Historically, hedonism made an important contribution to ethics by drawing attention to the importance of sensuality and pleasure in human experience. In the end, however, hedonism failed as a mature ethical philosophy because it was unable to transcend the immediacy and self-centeredness of the Impulsive stage.

One of the most important functions of the parenting culture is "to set limits on the child's behavior." This allows the child to recognize "the appropriate boundaries between himself and his parents," and "eventually between himself and his own impulses" (Kegan, 1982, p. 144). The most effective limit-setting, however, "is not merely about prevention, control, or the application of authority." Rather, it is:

> about the exercise of just those preventions, controls, or authorities which we can reasonably assume the developing person to next take over on her own. In this way, effective limit-setting both recognizes who the child is and who the child is becoming. (p. 145)

5.2. Later Childhood and Adolescence: The Imperial and Interpersonal Stages

As development moves from the Impulsive to the Imperial stage, the tension between attachment and autonomy is resolved in favor of autonomy. In this phase the child is "subject to" his or her needs, interests and wishes. The impulses of the Impulsive balance have become object, that is, the child has transcended his or her overly subjective embeddedness in his or her impulses.

The strength of this phase is a newly found "capacity to take command of one's impulses," that is, "a new sense of freedom, power, independence" (p. 89). The name of this phase refers to its limitation. In the Imperial stage there is an "absence of a shared reality" (p. 91). The immorally embedded self is not yet capable of a shared relationship, of mutuality or reciprocity. Others will often experience the person in this phase as manipulative and imperialistic. During the Imperial stage others are constituted by their ability to meet one's needs. "Instead of seeing my needs I see through my needs" (p. 91).

Guindon compares the ethical perspective of this stage with utilitarianism (1989a, pp. 76-82; 1992, pp. 72-78). Like hedonism, utilitarianism appreciates goodness in terms of pleasure and pain. It adds to this a quantitative evaluation of the consequences of human actions. This, as Guindon emphasizes, plays an important role in ethical reflection. It challenges overly idealistic philosophies to take into account the reality of concrete situations. Like the stage described by Kegan, however, it is imperialistic. It has difficulty relativizing immediate needs and reduces worthiness or goodness to that which is measurably useful.

In terms of sexual development, Kegan (1982) suggests that what we witness in this phase is not "a replay of the oedipal," (as Freud suggested) but two different periods which have common features. Again we witness the emergence from a balance that favored attachment to a balance that favors autonomy. On the supposedly quiet period of latency Kegan writes that "the whole notion of latency - of a Dark Ages in personality development - is one of Freud's least preservable constructions... there is a great deal going on during these years and not all of it is hidden" (p. 188). The culture of embeddedness in this phase now includes the family, school, and the peer group. The latter helps to culture the need for role differentiation and role-taking. The role of the family and school is to acknowledge and nurture the child's displays of self-sufficiency and competence. The second function (contradiction) becomes important as the preadolescent emerges "from embeddedness in self-sufficiency." Here the culture can help the child develop his or her "capacity for mutuality" by challenging the "validity of only taking one's interests into account." It must expect "trustworthiness" and demand "that the person hold up his or her end of relationship" (p. 119). As the early adolescent begins to move beyond the Imperial stage, he or she begins "to construct a world of mutuality and reciprocity" and is looking for "a holding environment that cultures its interpersonalism" (p. 167).

According to Kegan (1982), adolescence is characterized by the drive toward interpersonal mutuality. This drive has been referred to by others as a movement toward interpersonal affiliation, affection, love and belongingness, and reciprocity (p. 190). This is a time when persons experience a strong need to be connected or included in a "culture of mutuality," in one-to-one relationships.

The name of this phase refers to its strength. The new possibility of the Interpersonal balance is an openness to other that was not present in the Imperial balance. Mutuality defines the investments and commitments of a self that is now becoming "conversational" (p. 96).

Relationships and a concern for mutuality define the ground of one's knowing, being, and valuing.

The limitation of this stage is its overinclusiveness. One's entire self-cohesiveness is defined *through* relationships. In this stage "there is no self independent of the context of other people's liking." The person "lacks the self-coherence from space to space that is taken as the hallmark of identity" (p. 96). Persons in this phase, for example, have difficulty expressing anger. They "are more likely to feel sad, wounded, or incomplete... because they cannot know themselves separate from the interpersonal context" (p. 97). The evolving self at this stage is not yet fully interpersonal. As Guindon (1992) indicates, a more accurate name for this stage may be "fusional" (p. 87).

In the sexual domain the ethos that defines the self is not yet capable of full mutuality, reciprocity, and intimacy. It "can amount to an ethic of "my pleasure is your pleasure... what satisfies me is that you are satisfied" (Kegan, 1982, p. 204).

> This balance is "interpersonal" but it is not "intimacy," because what might appear to be intimacy here is the self's source rather than its aim. There is no self to share with another; instead the other is required to bring the self into being. If one can feel manipulated by the Imperial balance, one can feel devoured by the Interpersonal. (pp. 96-97)

The interpersonally embedded self is particularly vulnerable to a crisis in relationship, such as a break up or separation. The break up of an intimate relationship represents "the ultimate inability... to make myself cohere" (p. 192). It is an assault on the person at his or her core, his or her way of knowing/being/valuing. The person knows the world, exists in the world, and values through his or her investment in the interpersonal.

Loyalty to a person or a cause are critical at this stage (Guindon, 1989a, pp. 98-105; 1992, pp. 95-101). This is a new responsibility and possibility that was absent in the Imperial balance. The problem, however, is that the interpersonally embedded self tends to conform to the expectations of others (p. 95), and will naturally sacrifice his or her uniqueness to belong to the group (Keen, 1983). He or she lives through a cause the same way he or she may live through another person. Critical distance is extremely difficult for the person embedded in this stage.

According to Kegan, the cultures of embeddedness must resist the temptation to "advance" the person to the next stage. This is especially difficult in the Interpersonal balance. Given the priority Western culture places on individuation and autonomy, it is easy to deny the integrity of this stage. In due time the culture (one's conversational partners, parents, schools) will play an important role in recognizing and supporting the transition toward greater autonomy. The movement beyond fusion will be extremely difficult, however, if the culture fails first to recognize and celebrate the person's newly discovered ability to be conversational. It must acknowledge, support and nurture the "capacity for collaborative self-sacrifice" in interpersonal relationships and causes - no matter how imperfect that capacity may appear from an adult's perspective (Kegan, 1982, p. 191).

5.3. Adulthood: The Institutional and Interindividual Stages

As the Interpersonal evolves into the "Institutional," the self is becoming more autonomous and "political." The ultimacy of relationships is relativized and the person is becoming more self-regulating. The person "maintains a coherence across a shared psychological space and so achieves an identity" (p. 100). The new self is now capable of "coordinating and reflecting upon mutuality" (p. 100).

Ideology, form, law, and authority are the central motifs of this phase. The Institutional self is an administrator, and "regulation, rather than mutuality, is now ultimate" (p. 102). In the Interpersonal balance the main question was "Do you still like me?" In the Institutional balance the main question is "Does my government still stand?" (p. 102).

From an ethical perspective the evolving self at this stage is concerned with the ordering of individual rights and obligations. It is the responsibility of society and the legal system to safeguard and limit individual rights in light of the common good (Guindon, 1992, p. 113).

Kegan (1982) notes that social and cultural movements and ideologies can provide a culture of embeddedness which recognizes and holds the movement toward "a personally authored identity" (p. 213). "Whether the ideology is feminism or black power or gay rights," it can serve "the absolutely critical function of supporting the evolution of meaning" (p. 214). The women's movement is a good case in point.

Consciousness-raising groups, books about women's life changes, and story, song, and slogan do far more than mutually confirm one's experience or let one know that one is not alone. They actually do raise consciousness (which is what evolution is all about) exactly because they sponsor a qualitative reconstruction of the self and the world. The women's movement offers invitations to women to see the very fact of their womenhood as entry to the ideological participation which is essential to the institutional evolutionary balance. (p. 213)

As the Institutional stage begins to wear itself thin, the person begins to realize that there is something beyond form, structure and ideology. There begins to emerge "a kind of sharing or intimacy with others that has not been present since the Interpersonal stage. This new stage (which Kegan labels "Interindividual"), however, is different from the Interpersonal stage "in the sense that the intimacy which is possible in the new balance, is the self's aim rather than its source" (p. 238).

The new possibility and strength of this stage is its capacity for self-authorship. Each person maintains his or her distinct identity. "The evolutionary gains of institutionality, while transformed, are nonetheless preserved (the love is not captive of the identity, but neither is the identity lost)" (p. 253). This post-ideological transformation, says Kegan, sets the stage for intimacy.

The task of this transformation is to "transcend the tyranny of the form" (p. 247). This task "may evidence itself cognitively in terms of dialectical thought, or sociomorally in terms of a post-ideological construction" and "in the wider arena of the psychological self as the capacity for genuine intimacy" (p. 253).

In sexuality one does not subordinate "one's pleasure to the other's." One satisfies oneself by transcending "in resplendent play, the isolation of our separateness..." (p. 253). Ethically speaking, the dignity of the human person becomes more important than the ordering of obligations (Guindon, 1989a, p. 143). Here Kegan (1982), much like Gilligan, suggests "that there is qualitative development beyond psychological autonomy and philosophical formalism" (p. 228).

Reciprocity now becomes a matter of at once mutually preserving the other's distinctiveness while interdependently fashioning a bigger context in which these separate identities interpenetrate, by

> which the separate identities are co-regulated, and to which persons invest an affection supervening their separate identities. Reciprocity now becomes a matter of both holding and being held, a mutual protection of each partner, an opportunity to experience and exercise both sides of life's fundamental tension. (p. 254)

The culture of embeddedness in this stage (which includes the domain of love and work) must acknowledge and culture the "capacity for interdependence, for self-surrender and intimacy, for interdependent self-definition" (p. 227). The problem here, as Kegan suggests, is that "work settings which can encourage, recognize, or support development beyond the institutional are quite rare." The work place tends to exist "for the purpose of maintaining the organization" and has little interest in intimate "self-exploration," and the "possible reconstruction of its goals" (p. 244). The traditional workplace is likely to "overhold ideological adulthood just as surely as a mother and father can overhold a five-year-old" (p. 245).

Although Kegan himself does not fully explore the ethical meanings of this stage, I believe that its basic metaphors suggest an ecological ethic. An ecological ethic takes the idea of the interpenetration of self systems to include all forms of life, human and non-human. Its main focus of attention shifts from rights, obligations and freedoms to a concern with the interconnectedness of all life. A person animated by this ethic understands that the earth holds us as much as we hold it. In *The Passionate Life* Sam Keen (1983) summarizes the essential characteristics of this ethic. In the following passage, which will be quoted at length, Keen effectively contrasts the liberal ethic of rights which was criticized in chapter three of this book with an ecological ethic. For Keen an ecological ethic is the ethic of a radical "lover."

> The liberal mind is always seeking to grant or recognize the rights of some previously disenfranchised minority. To recognize that trees and timber wolves have a claim to justice is an extension of granting rights to women, children, blacks, and homosexuals. Where the question of rights and justice is in the foreground, the question of love has not yet been raised with seriousness. The liberal fights for someone else's rights. By contrast, the radical or the lover understands that all society is bound together in such a way that if anyone's rights are denied, we are all imprisoned. It is not for the poor wolves that we demand rights - but for ourselves.

The liberal mind defines and tries to solve problems from a position *exterior* to them: I'm OK (free, healthy, enlightened, educated, enfranchised), but my neighbor is not. The radical mind of the lover tries to heal dis-ease from a position *interior* to it: Neither you nor I can be free or healthy, until both of us live in a liberated community. To the liberal mind, the land is a thing for which we are responsible; animals are lower species we should respect. To the radical mind, land, animals, and people are relatives with whom we cohabit, members of a communion of sentient beings bound together by the demands of kindness. (pp. 235-236; cf. 1991, pp. 116-122; Cairns, 1990; Moran, 1987, pp. 36-42)

Table 5.1 outlines Kegan's stages. It includes the culture of embeddedness, the psychologic and ethic of each stage.

Table 5.1. Kegan's Stages of Development

Stage	Culture	Psychologic	Ethic
Incorporative	Mothering	Attachment	
Impulsive	Parenting	Attachment	Hedonism
Imperial	Family, School, Peer Group	Autonomy	Utilitarian
Interpersonal	Partners, Parents, School	Attachment	Loyalty
Institutional	Work, Ideology	Autonomy	Legalist
Inter-individual	Love, Work	Autonomy & Attachment	Ecological

CHAPTER 6

Educational Principles and Issues Arising

This chapter examines: 1) what it means to teach values responsibly in light of Kegan's theory on the cultures of embeddedness; 2) the importance of narrative and storytelling for sexual-values education; and 3) the need to reconceptualize sexual-values education as a life-long process.

6.1. Teaching Values: The Creative Tension Between Receptivity and Confrontation

As was seen in chapter two, the ethic of value-neutrality represents an attempt to move beyond the moralizing instinct of previous approaches to sexuality education. Because values are seen as personal and subjective, and because we live in a pluralistic society, proponents of Values Clarification argue that the teacher's role is to clarify and affirm, rather than change or challenge, the values of their students.

Proponents of Values Clarification recognize that teaching responsibly is first and foremost about creating a welcoming space that allows teachers and students to explore value questions without fear of ridicule (cf. Nouwen, 1975, p. 60). No one will share their values in a hostile climate. If values represent our most fundamental convictions, and if values are intimately connected to who we are as persons, to have our values attacked is to be challenged at the level of our identity and integrity as persons.

Values education requires an environment of openness, humility, and mutual trust; an environment where "there is excitement without threat, exploration without the desire to win points or the need to convert the other" (Carter, 1984, p. 138). Without this openness and trust, dialogue is replaced by debate and by attempts to make others look ignorant or foolish. Form taking precedence over content, performance over truth, argumentation over dialogue, and domination and humiliation over insight and growth (Morris, 1988).

Values Clarification represents a significant achievement in sexuality education. It is not, as some would claim, a sign of moral decline. Recognizing the importance of respecting diverging viewpoints, as well as the importance of respecting the integrity of persons, it is underlied by a powerful moral ideal (cf. Taylor, 1991). As was seen in chapter two, the problem with Values Clarification is that it confuses subjectivity with subjectivism, pluralism with relativism, and integrity with validity.

According to Kegan's theory, moral growth is enhanced, not by neutrality, but through the interplay of affirmation (receptivity) and contradiction (confrontation). Moral growth largely depends on the presence of a qualitative holding environment that affirms and celebrates the integrity of a person's present way of knowing, being, and valuing. It also depends on the presence of appropriate and timely confrontation. Confrontation allows the valuing subject to transcend the limitations of his or her present epistemological and ethical constructions; to assess critically the validity of "made meanings."

Many teachers are uncomfortable with the idea of confrontation because it conjures images of verbal warfare. Seen from the perspective of Kegan's theory, genuine confrontation is really about creating limits and boundaries which allow teachers and students (or parents and children) to search for, discover, and evaluate their respective subjectivities. As Nouwen (1975) writes:

> To be receptive to the stranger in no way implies that we have to become neutral "nobodies." Real receptivity asks for confrontation because space can only be a welcoming space when there are clear boundaries, and boundaries are limits between which we define our own position. Flexible limits, but limits nonetheless... We are not hospitable when we leave our house to strangers and let them use it any way they want. An empty house is not a hospitable house... it quickly becomes a ghost house... No real dialogue is possible between somebody and a nobody. We can enter into communication with the other only when our life choices, attitudes and viewpoints offer the boundaries that challenge strangers to

become aware of their own position and to explore it critically. (pp. 69-70)

When teaching is seen as a dialectical tension between receptivity and confrontation, effective teaching may sometimes call for some form of preaching. Preaching in an appropriate context can challenge persons to reflect more deeply on their most influential presuppositions. As Gabriel Moran (1987) indicates, "Unlikely characters such as Adolf Hitler or Reverend Jim Jones get a place in history books for mesmerizing people with sermons. But the positive possibilities are evident in the speeches of Roosevelt or Churchill, King or Ghandi" (p. 153). "Despite its domestication within the institution," notes Moran, preaching can have a constructive and liberating effect "when it is filled with wit and irony, turning upside down what is assumed to be normal morality, the morality of complacency and self-congratulation" (p. 154).

Moran's reference to wit and irony is particularly important for sexual-values education. Humor, as Daniel Maguire (1978) writes:

> jolts our bowed head back and makes us look up to discover that little plot of reality on which we had been gazing with fixed vision is bounded by a universe. Humor bespeaks more. In humor we leap beyond the limits of our reasonable conceptions and taste something of the more that is always beckoning beyond. (p. 351)

In *Harvard Diary* Robert Coles tells an anecdote which offers an interesting insight into why we may have turned entirely against preaching. Coles recalls one of his elementary school teachers who would frequently tell the class that they should "try hard to practice what they preached." One day an astute pupil asked the teacher "whether those who don't preach really have any reason to be worried - since, after all, they are not hypocrites" (1990, p. 167). This clever grade five pupil sensed that not preaching saves us from having to be accountable; that remaining neutral can become an effective means of escaping the courage of our convictions.

Speech is not the only way to confront and challenge. Genuine confrontation can also occur through moments of silence and through the discipline of contemplative solitude. Moments of silence in a conversation can be as important to the conversation as the words and arguments. It allows those engaged in a dialogue to stop, reflect, and be present to what is *really* being said. Those teachers and students who speak incessantly take control of the learning environment (Palmer, 1983, pp. 80-81). They violate the space that makes fearless dialogue and communication possible. "Silence," as holocaust survivor Elie Wiesel says, "is the soul of the word" (cited in Bonisteel, 1980, p. 54; cf. De Smedt, 1986).

Silence and speech, like separation and connection, are two poles within the same process. Just as we must separate to find more expanded forms of connection, surrender control to find autonomy and gain control, we must pause in silence to speak truthfully. In solitude and silence, confrontation is confrontation with self, a time to be "inwardly attentive" (Lindbergh, 1978, p. 56; cf. Palmer, 1983, pp. 121-124; Storr, 1988). Contemplation through solitude is necessary to "unveil the illusions that masquerade as reality and reveal the reality behind the masks" (Palmer, 1990, p. 17). We need to cultivate the discipline of solitude, as Keen (1991) says, "to acquire a heartful mind" (p. 160).

> Solitude begins when (we) silence the competing voices of the market, the polis, the home, the mass, and listen to the dictates of (our) own heart. Self-love requires the same commitment of time and energy as any other relationship. I must take time to be with myself, to discover my own desires, my rhythms, my tastes, my gifts, my hopes, my wounds. (p. 161)

This attentiveness has nothing to do with selfishness or "navel gazing." Contemplative solitude "does not pull us away from our fellow human beings but instead makes real fellowship possible" (Nouwen, 1975, p. 28). Dietrich Bonhoeffer, a theologian who was arrested and executed for his opposition to Nazism, wrote extraordinary letters on fellowship and justice while in solitary confinement (Bethge, 1972). "It is in deep solitude," wrote Thomas Merton in the last years of his life, "that I find gentleness with which I can truly love my brothers. The more solitary I am, the more affection I have for them. It is pure affection and filled with reverence for the solitude of others" (cited in Nouwen, 1975, p. 28).

6.2. The Importance of Narrative and Storytelling for Sexual-Values Education

This section examines the educational value of narrative and storytelling. Narrative and storytelling place meaning, understanding, and the moral imagination at the center of the educational process. They provide powerful and effective ways of affirming the integrity of persons and of challenging the validity of made meanings. They also hold considerable promise as alternatives to value clarification exercises, hypothetical moral dilemmas, and approaches that polarize value questions as either/or issues.

I have always been fascinated by the power of storytelling. Simple words like "have I told you the story about..." can cast a magic spell which triggers a fever of excitement and expectation. It is wonderful to see how a good story can infuse life back into facial expressions which have been worn down by hours of lecturing and note taking. Time and time again I have heard elementary and high school teachers describe how an uninterested and unruly class was transformed by telling a story, and how some students, much to the teachers' surprise, will even say "thank you" for sharing a story.

For many people storytelling is merely a form of entertainment, a technique to keep students attentive. I recall working with a student-teacher who had difficulty accepting the fact that the only time his students really listened to him was when he told stories. "I can not entertain them all the time!," he said in exasperation. "I have to get on with the curriculum!"

This teacher failed to appreciate the epistemological value of storytelling. There is no doubt that a good tale told by an able story teller is very entertaining. More is going on, however, than mere entertainment. At a deeper level storytelling helps us to make sense of our experience. We do not tell stories simply because they are more entertaining than arguments or ideas, but because they offer opportunities for self-understanding. They alone have the power to fully articulate, order and unify the richness and complexity of our actual lived experience (Tracy, 1986, p. 275; cf. Blakely, 1988; Bruner, 1986; Egan, 1986a, 1988; Polakow, 1986). As Stanley Hauerwas (1977) writes:

> A story, thus, is a narrative account that binds events and agents together in an intelligible pattern. We do not tell stories simply

because they provide us a more colorful way to say what can be said in a different way, but because there is no other way we can articulate the richness of intentional activity - that is, behavior that is purposeful but not necessary. For any good novelist knows that there is always more involved in any human action than can be said. To tell a story often involves our attempt to make intelligible the muddle of things we have done in order to have a self. (p. 76)

Judy Bloom's book (1986) *Letters to Judy: What Kids Wish They Could Tell You* provides many illustrations of the role narrative can play in meaning-making and self-understanding. The book, which is a compilation of letters written by Bloom's readers, deals with issues ranging from teenage suicide and pregnancy to puberty and homosexuality. These letters, which are narratives in themselves, provide remarkable insights into the spiritual and moral struggles of young people today. (Adult readers might find some of these letters more illuminating than many of the psychological theories on adolescence.)

An interesting feature of these letters is how Bloom's readers ask her if she could please write them a story about their particular concern. They never ask for information on the so-called "facts of life" or for decision-making techniques. They rarely ask for direct advice or for solutions to problems. Experience has taught them that what they really need is a good story, one that will make more palpable the struggle to make sense of their particular quandary. They know that "all sorrows," as Isak Dinesen says, "can be borne if we put them into a story or if you tell a story about them" (cited in Keen & Valley-Fox, 1989, p. 1).

Without a story the "facts of life," and the decisions we make, become vacuous. As Postman (1989) writes:

A story provides a structure for our perceptions; only through stories do facts assume any meaning whatsoever. This is why children everywhere ask, as soon as they have the command of language to do so, "Where did I come from?" and, shortly after, "What will happen when I die?" They require a story to give meaning to their existence... Without a story people have no idea what to do with information. They cannot even tell what is information and what is not. (pp. 122-123; cf. Moran, 1983a, p. 199)

Another interesting feature of the letters to Judy is how her readers offer to tell their own stories. This is consistent with how we make sense of significant experiences in our lives. In recounting an important experience or event we do not merely compile a list of facts about the experience. We tell a story about it by situating the experience in a particular time and place, and within a network of relations. We know that the listener(s) will not be able to really understand what happened, and particularly how we felt about what happened, unless we describe the circumstances surrounding the experience, unless we tell the *whole* story.

Telling the story allows one to further organize the experience into some sort of recognizable and meaningful pattern. Telling a story about a significant *moral* experience provides an opportunity for deepening one's reflection on that experience (Tappan & Brown, 1991, p. 182). It provides a way of imposing "form upon our often chaotic experiences, and in the process, to develop our own voice. Listening to our own stories is a way for us to nourish, encourage and sustain ourselves" (Cooper, 1991, p. 97).

The process of authoring one's story is at once a way of caring for ourselves, a way of sustaining moral reflection, and "a way out of helplessness into a kind of personal power" (p. 107). It helps us to break through oppressive forms of silence "that prevent us from being fully present to ourselves" (p. 107), and as a result, that prevent us from taking responsibility for our actions (Tappan & Brown, 1991, p. 184). Telling our own story provides us with opportunities to *evaluate critically* the stories we live by. Unless we become conscious of the myths that inform our values, we are in danger, as Keen (1988) argues, "of being dominated by them" (p. 45).

The story's capacity to provide encouragement and nourishment is particularly important. A good story allows us to be who we are, and gives us the energy and courage to go on (Hauerwas, 1980; Coles, 1986, 1989). As Kegan (1982) notes, story and storytelling can "mutually confirm one's experience," "let one know that one is not alone," and "raise consciousness" (p. 213). They serve as cultures of embeddedness, holding us and much as we hold them (cf. Lopez, 1990, p. 48). Storytelling, in other words, is a powerful means of affirming the integrity and identity of persons. As Polkinghorne (1988) writes, "we achieve our personal identities and self-concept" by seeing our life "as an expression of a single unfolding and developing story." Self "is not a static thing or a substance, but a configuring of personal events into an historical unity which includes not only what one has been but also anticipations of what one will be" (1988 p. 150; cf. Bruner, 1990, pp. 111-116). We must, therefore, as Keen argues, help individuals form the "raw materials of [their] own experience into a coherent story." "Since we live out of a past and toward a future, it is difficult to see how human integrity could be possible without memory or hope, without placing the present moment within a temporal context, without telling a story" (1970, p. 71).

The experience of telling and *sharing* our stories can also create a sense of intimacy and community among persons. A teacher once told me a story that provides a good illustration of this. She was teaching a novel in a high school English class and had considerable difficulty getting the students to cooperate. The situation began to change when she asked them to share the sections of the novel they enjoyed most. With each story the students spontaneously moved closer and closer together, until by the end of the class, they were huddled in a small circle. Sharing the part *they* enjoyed most gave them an opportunity to share a little bit of their own stories. Sharing their own stories allowed them to bridge some of their differences, and thereby develop a sense of connection with each other. As Witherell (1991) writes, narrative in education provides opportunities "deepened understanding of others and for bridging morally diverse communities" (p. 239).

Furthermore, giving people the opportunity to tell and share their own stories saves the ethic of decision-making from its presumptuousness. It allows us to see that meanings and decisions are not things we make on our own. Narrative and storytelling show how meanings and decisions are revealed, discovered, made and negotiated in a context of human interaction.

Stories, whether fictional or "real life", can also challenge the valuing subject to transcend the limitations of his or her made meanings. Well-told stories engage the moral imagination in a dialogue between that is and what might be. It urges the valuing subject to expand his or her horizon.

Tragedy can play an important role in this process. The tragic story, as Maguire (1978) writes, "is a voice from the real world." It "enters with its shocking newness and tears at our psychic structures and habitations." Tragedy "is a powerful reminder that all is not as we had imagined." It "introduces a new horizon" (p. 363).

The tragic story allows us to actually *feel* the trials and tribulations of *real* human beings. Enfleshing morality in living persons and real life experiences, it has the capacity to reach deep down inside and touch our most basic emotions and values. Tragedy, unlike value clarification exercises or hypothetical moral dilemmas, has the power to move us, and to heighten our sense of compassion for others. Tragedy, like comedy, "ruptures cold complacency and offers our moral consciousness a chance for healing" (Maguire, 1978, p. 358; cf. Johnson, 1993, p. 200).

Since 1983 I have been involved in a university course called "Values and Human Sexuality" (see Lawlor, et al., 1990). A few years ago a person living with AIDS was invited to be a guest speaker in one of the classes. His presentation included statistics on HIV/AIDS, as well as a list of risk behaviors. What remained most with the students, however, was his story. Their encounter with this man's story showed them the human face of AIDS. It taught them that AIDS is far more than a disease or a statistic. It challenged their assumptions and presuppositions about persons with AIDS. They experienced compassion, or what Maguire refers to as "the foundational moral experience," that is, the experience of the sacredness of persons (pp. 72-79). In our next class meeting, one student who had never met anyone with AIDS before, said, "I just can't get him out of my mind. He is still with me and will remain with me for a long time."

As was seen in chapter three, Kohlberg defines morality in terms of competing claims, and moral agency as deliberation, judgment and decision-making. The tragic story introduces the valuing subject to a different level of moral reflection. It situates the moral agent in what Gilligan describes as an ethic of interpretation, dialogue, and responsiveness to human need. The main question arising from the story I describe above is not "How can I resolve two conflicting claims?" but rather "How can I care for this person?" The story challenges our moral imaginations to consider how we might respond most humanly to this particular person, and how we might contribute to making this world a better place for persons living with AIDS.

Many of the moral issues in sexuality call for this type of moral reflection. At the beginning of the "Values and Human Sexuality" course the students are told that their papers can address any topic that interests them as long as the papers include reflections on the ethical questions and issues central to that topic. Those who are thinking of doing a paper on pornography know immediately how to approach their paper. They will focus on the arguments for and against pornography. Those who are interested in doing a paper on an area like the sexual abuse of children, however, are confused. They usually say something like: "How can my paper include an elaborate discussion of ethical issues and questions when the sexual abuse of children is obviously wrong?" Having been educated to see morality as competing claims and as either/or issues, they have difficulty seeing the ethical questions arising.

Some of the questions we encourage them to examine include: Do we have a responsibility to intervene in the lives of children whom we know are victims of sexual abuse? How should we intervene? How can we most effectively and humanly respond to a child's disclosure? Should we seek help? How can we empower children to protect themselves without scaring them? How can we "street proof" without "life-proofing?" Is there something we can do about the social structures and practices which perpetuate sexual abuse?

These questions begin to make sense when the students are introduced to stories about survivors of sexual abuse. The statistics on abuse give them a sense of how widespread the phenomenon actually is. The stories allow them to *feel with* the abused person. Those who have been victims themselves are given permission to come out of their isolation. Those who have not been victims themselves, or at least who have not been deeply scarred by an abusive situation, begin to feel empathy, compassion, and sometimes moral outrage. It is here that the questions of responsibility, accountability and action begin welling up within them.

Narrative and storytelling, therefore, are not merely pedagogical devices to keep students attentive. They are important for sexual-values education because they put meaning, understanding and imagination at the center of the educational process. Storytelling is a fundamental way of discerning and discovering patterns of meaning which can illuminate and guide our lives. The imaginative patterns of stories are invitations to transcendence. They stimulate the moral imagination and heighten our sense of compassion for others. The opportunity to tell and share our own stories puts us in touch with the unity, integrity, and relationality of our lives. It helps us move from isolation to a sense of intimacy and interconnectedness.

> Whether biographical or fictional, stories provide meaning and belonging in our lives. They attach us to others, to our history, and to ourselves by providing a tapestry rich with threads of time, place, character, and even advice on what we might do with our lives. The

story fabric offers us images, myths, and metaphors that are morally
resonant and contribute both to our knowing and our being known.
(Witherell, 1991, p. 239)

6.3. Sexual-Values Education as a Life Long Process

As was seen in the first two chapters, sexuality education has been
consistently conceptualized as a possible solution to problems like
unwanted teenage pregnancy and STDs. The problem with this view is
that it conceptualizes sexuality education as an *object* in the *school*
curriculum which does or does not produce certain *effects* (Moran,
1983b). In this paradigm the value of sexuality education is measured
by standards which are exclusively *quantitative* and *utilitarian*.

The issues raised in this book lead to a totally different way of
thinking about sexuality education. Kegan's theory suggests that sexual-
values education is not an object in school, but rather a process that
spans an entire life-time. Education, as Moran (1987) argues:

> is not a *product* available in school as is commonly assumed. Education
> is not a *wider thing* than school so that education would emerge as the
> school walls are lowered. Education *is a different kind of reality from
> school or schooling*. While school is a definite institution, and schooling
> is a particular form of learning, *education is not a thing at all but a
> lifetime process constituted by a set of relations*. (p. 12)

Kegan's theory on the cultures of embeddedness suggests that
sexual-values education occurs not only in the school, but also in the
mothering culture, in play, the family, peer groups, one-to-one
relationships, and the work place (cf. Moran, 1989, pp. 237-242). In the
Incorporative stage, for example, the "mothering" culture's capacity
literally to "hold" is the first educational response that allows persons to
humanize their sexuality. Although the Piagetian paradigm sees this
stage as pre-moral, the stage is nonetheless rich in moral meanings and
implications. As was seen in chapter five, holding nurtures the child's
capacity for intimacy, independence, and non-violent interpersonal
relations.

In the "parenting culture," sexual-values education continues
through the celebration of the child's capacity for fantasy. The contact
with mythic stories acquaints children with basic emotions and values;
with the tensions between love and hate, security and fear, courage and

cowardice, good and bad (Egan, 1986b, pp. 12-13; cf. Moran, 1983a, pp. 176-177). Adult injunctions to be "practical" and "realistic" deny children their most basic way of understanding morality.

Sexual-values education in this stage also occurs through the education of the senses. As Guindon (1986) emphasizes, the integration of one's sexuality "hinges not solely on the quality of human values family members believe in and seek to implement in their lives, but also on the sophistication of their sensory equipment" (p. 126). Through the family meal, children are introduced "to tastes, odors, colors, forms." "The disappearance of this activity leaves one skeptical about the success of sexual education. How does one educate without the basics?" (pp. 126-127; cf. Ackerman, 1991).

In the Interpersonal stage, sexual-values education continues through the affirmation and celebration of the person's newly discovered ability to be conversational; the ability to commit to a reality outside of oneself. Just as "holding" empowers the child to move out into the world, recognizing and supporting the Interpersonal self's emerging capacity for self-sacrifice empowers the adolescent or young adult to move toward a more balanced view of intimacy and mutuality.

When seen in this manner the value of sexuality education is no longer determined by its capacity to produce quantifiable outcomes, but rather by its capacity to be celebrational, edifying and life-enhancing. The main question is no longer whether a particular program or approach did or did not have a certain effect; but rather, how can we improve the quality of our overall educational experience? How can sexuality education facilitate, support, and critically assist persons in their search for moral integrity and coherence? Rather than focus constantly on the possible effects of a teenager's sexual behavior, it becomes much more important to ask whether the "culture of mutuality" has successfully celebrated that person's newly discovered capacity to be conversational? Does the culture recognize the movement from fusion to autonomy and self-authorship?

In adulthood, does the work place support and acknowledge the Institutional self's capacity for independence, and does it recognize the movement toward interindividuality? And who will culture the cultures of embeddedness? For example, can the mothering culture, particularly in single parent families, adequately support the child's need to be held without the support of an extended family, without the mother herself being held? Can single mothers provide an adequate "holding environment" if they are exhausted by the struggle for financial survival?   In other words, is sexual education possible without restructuring the gender order (see Naus, 1989, 1991)?

The idea that sexuality education is life-long is not new.   The meanings and actual implications of this concept, however, have yet to be taken seriously. If we really mean education and not just schooling, and if we accept that education is a life-long process "constituted by a set of relations," then we must begin to see sexuality education as a shared responsibility. We have to stop expecting that schoolteachers will, by themselves, solve complex social problems. If we really accept that sexuality education is life-long, then we have to attend more fully to the needs and concerns of those who have yet to begin school and those who are not yet dead - but who may be older, disabled, ill or dying.

The reconceptualization of sexuality education as a life-long process also challenges us to expand our concept of "teacher training" to include those teachers who are not professional schoolteachers. It challenges us to examine how children might participate in the sexuality education of their parents, how the disabled or ill might educate the able bodied and healthy, and how the elderly might participate in the sexuality education of young children.

> The very young and the very old are co-conspirators in a world obsessed with rational productivity. Beneath the differences in the number of wrinkles and the amount of physical energy, the old and the young, if given half a chance, discover a common good. Anyone whose theory of education does not include a grandparent sitting quietly in the sunlight does not have an adequate theory. If the world has a future at all, that future largely depends upon the child a few years from birth and the old person a few years from death speaking, in their own secretive way, of mysteries that the rest of the race is too old or too young to comprehend. (Moran, 1983a, p. 182; cf. 1989, pp. 233-237)

The following tables propose a preliminary sketch for a life-span view of sexual-values education. The tables outline three levels of sexuality education based on Kegan's stages. Kegan's theory on the cultures of embeddedness helps to focus the educational meanings and responsibilities of each stage. The characteristics of the three levels are also informed by Egan's (1986b) stages of educational development and Moran's (1983a) interpretation of these stages in his theory of religious education development.

Table 6.1. Sexual-Values Education From Childhood to Early Adulthood

Stages	Educational Site	Modes of Learning & Living	Modes of Teaching & Educating
I. Sexual Education			
1.Incorporative to Impulsive	mothering culture	senses, reflexes	literally holding
2.Impulsive to Imperial	parenting culture, family, school	senses, play, fantasy, language, family rituals, T.V.	fantasy: tales, songs, puppets, games, humanizing senses
II. Sex(y) Education			
3.Imperial to Interpersonal	peers, family, school	interpersonal relations, fusion	role playing, "realistic" stories, celebrate capacity for attachment
4.Interpersonal to Institutional	school, peers, work	distancing, critique	culture capacity for autonomy, space to critique, opportunities to tell own story

Table 6.2.   Sexual-Values Education in Adulthood and
Later Life

Stages	Educational Site	Modes of Learning & Living	Modes of Teaching & Educating
III. Sexual Education			
5.Instit-utional to Inter-individual	work, family, community	novels, movies, T.V., parenting	support groups, ironic humor, biography, auto-biography
6.Inter-individual to Leisurely	family, community, places of leisure, health care institutes	sense of vulnerability, playful sensuality	poetry, courses in massage, teaching youth, institutional support (intimacy)

The two tables summarize many of the issues raised in this chapter
and situate different narrative forms across the stages. It is important to
emphasize, however, that each narrative form, as well as each
educational site and responsibility, is not exclusive to the particular stage
in which it is listed. The tables highlight a context, form, or task that is
particularly appropriate at that stage.

The term "sexual education" in the first level highlights the task of
sensual incorporation and the need to humanize the senses in the first
two stages. The term "sex(y)" education in the second level refers to the
biological transformations that occur in the Imperial and Interpersonal
stages, as well as the extraordinary investment the Interpersonally
embedded self makes in how he or she looks through the eyes of others.

The term "sexual education" in the third level highlights the return of sensuality as both a mode of learning and teaching. All three stages require each other. This is especially true of the first and last stages. Infants' capacity to incorporate their sensuality largely depends on adults' capacity to be sensual.

Since Kegan has little to say about aging and the experience of later life, I have added Moran's (1983a) "leisurely" stage. Moran is one of the few theorists who addresses educational issues in later life. Moran suggests that the leisurely stage may be a time for a return to school. People "who have retired or partially withdrawn from their jobs" are "ready now for books and ideas to clarify their fund of experience." The word "school," as Moran notes, "comes from the Greek word for leisure" (p. 181).

If I were to devise a sexual education curriculum for persons in their later life I would also include courses in massage. Courses in massage given in a reputable school, and by formally trained teachers, could have at least three major benefits. First, it could help older persons discover the sensual potential of their entire bodies, and provide an opportunity to demythologize the myth of coitus. Second, it could empower them to meet the young child's need to be held and touched. This would allow them to share the educational responsibilities of the first stage. Third, the possibility of receiving and giving massages could help persons move out of the physical isolation and sense of uselessness that becomes so tragically part of their experience as they get older.

If the idea of giving courses in massage for elderly persons sounds a bit strange, this may be because tender and sensual touch have been absent from our own educational experience. It may also underscore the extent to which we have difficulty perceiving older persons as sensual-sexual beings. Unfortunately, we also tend to associate massage with massage parlors and prostitution.

Courses in massage could, but need not, include full bodied massage. They could include sessions on how to give a simple back, neck, or hand massage. To paraphrase Moran (1983a, p. 182), we might say that anyone whose theory of sexual education does not include a grandparent gently stroking a child's back does not have an adequate theory. Allowing the very young and very old to literally get "in touch" with each other might, in the words of Sam Keen (1970), "help fill the vacuum within and between persons which is now cluttered with words. We might then, as they say in Maine, speak only when we could improve on silence" (p. 46).

None of this will be possible, however, unless health care institutions, "homes" for the elderly, and families recognize and support the aging person's continued need for independence and intimacy. The success of sexual education in later life, like in all stages, requires individual, community, and institutional support.

A life-span approach to sexual-values education will also have limited success if the growing awareness of child sexual abuse leads to a paranoia about all forms of touching. Awareness of child sexual abuse is a major achievement. It has led to educational programs and laws designed to protect children from abuse. Sexual education is in trouble, however, if this awareness also leads to an anti-touch mentality, and if touching becomes synonymous with abuse. How can an adult sit "quietly" and gently stroke a child's back if he or she is dominated by the fear of abusing? How can children recognize an abusive touch, say "no" to that touch, and avoid situations which make them vulnerable, if they have never experienced a qualitative holding and touching environment? Again, how can we educate without the basics?

CONCLUSION

Sexuality education in the late 19th and early 20th centuries was highly prescriptive and moralistic. The organized campaigns promoting school programs, as well as the popular advice literature, saw all non-marital and non-procreative sexual behavior as either immoral or unhealthy. The underlying philosophy of sexuality was deeply pessimistic and the main educational objective was to solve sexual-moral problems like unwanted teenage pregnancy, prostitution, and STDs.

The call for value-freedom which characterized the 1960s was an attempt to free sexuality education from its sexual pessimism and moralizing instinct. In the 1970s, and particularly in the 1980s, we begin to see a growing consensus on the need to address values. Approaches to sexuality education which separate fact and value are seen as inadequate and ineffective.

From the 1980s to the present, Values Clarification is the most popular approach to values in sexuality education. Here values and valuing are seen as personal and subjective, and the teacher's role is defined primarily in terms of value-neutrality. Although proponents of Values Clarification reject the idea that sexuality education can and should be value-free, they do emphasize that the teacher should remain neutral and merely help clarify the values of their students.

The 1980s also saw the emergence of a strong reactionary critique of Values Clarification. Representatives of right wing political and religious organizations vociferously attacked Values Clarification arguing that it undermines the authority of parents, promotes "promiscuity," and attempts to change or manipulate the values of students.

This reactionary critique, coupled with the growing pluralism of North American society, has reinforced the commitment to value-neutrality. Proponents of values in sexuality education are careful to avoid any position or strategy that would attempt to inculcate values. Neutrality is seen as necessary to ensure objectivity, and to ensure that teachers respect the integrity of different value positions.

This book has also presented a critique of Values Clarification. Unlike the reactionary critiques, however, the book has argued that Values Clarification marks a significant advance in the history of sexuality education. Proponents of Values Clarification are committed to an important moral ideal. They correctly recognize the need to affirm the subjectivity and integrity of the valuing subject, and to respect the growing pluralism of values.

The problem with Values Clarification is that it fails to distinguish subjectivity from subjectivism, integrity from validity, and pluralism from relativism. While it is true that values have a personal and subjective dimension, and that we need to respect the growing pluralism of values, it does not follow that value positions cannot be compared and critically evaluated. Kegan's theory suggests that the primary challenge of sexual-values education is not to clarify those values "already there," and to remain neutral, but to find ways of *challenging* the validity of value positions without *attacking* the integrity of the valuing subject. Sexual-values education promotes moral growth and transformation when it affirms and confronts. Genuine confrontation, one that challenges rather than attacks, can occur through dialogue, preaching, contemplative silence, and through story and storytelling. Storytelling may be one of the most powerful means of affirming and confronting.

Furthermore, the idea that objectivity is best served by neutrality is epistemologically naive. It assumes the existence of a special place outside of language and history where one can be free of prior value commitments. Objectivity is achieved, not by neutrality, but when teachers consciously seek out their value commitments and reflect on how these commitments shape their teaching.

Lawrence Kohlberg's theory of moral development and education represents a viable alternative to Values Clarification. Its developmental and principled approach to moral issues offers a way beyond neutrality and subjectivism. There are problems, however, with Kohlberg's reduction of morality to competing claims and rights, and with his reduction of moral agency to autonomy and formal decision-making. As Gilligan argues, Kohlberg abstracts the narrative from moral life.

While the literature's philosophical orientation on values has changed considerably over the past three decades, the underlying philosophy of sexuality education has remained constant. Ever since the first organized campaigns of the late 19th century, sexuality education has been conceptualized as a solution to problems like unwanted teenage pregnancy and STDs. The difficulty with this view is that it associates sexuality exclusively with moral problems and diseases. An adequate sexual-values education needs to recover the goodness and beauty of human sexuality.

The conceptualization of sexuality education as a solution to sexual-moral problems also rests on a reductionistic and instrumental view of sexuality education. Education is reduced to schooling, and the value of sexual-values education is determined by its capacity to produce quantifiable outcomes. In this book I have used Kegan's life-span view of development, and particularly his theory on the cultures of embeddedness, to propose a more holistic view of sexual-values education. The life-span view outlined in chapter six suggests that the school is only one among many educational sites, that education in sexuality is a shared responsibility, that sexual-values education begins at least at birth and does not end until death, and that the value of sexuality education is determined by its capacity to be celebrational, hospitable, meaningful, and life-enhancing.

As was suggested in chapter six, however, the complete details of a life-span view of sexual-values education still await careful research. The model outlined in tables 6.1 and 6.2 represent a preliminary sketch. Areas that need to be developed further include the nature and organization of sexuality education in adulthood and in later life, as well as the appropriateness of different narrative forms at different stages in the life-cycle. There is a need for research, for example, which examines the experience and impact of oral storytelling versus movies and novels, and of research which studies the relative importance of writing and sharing one's own story in adolescence and adulthood.

Teacher "training" is another area that needs to be explored more fully. How can university faculties of education adequately prepare people to teach sexual-values education? What kinds of courses should they offer? How should these courses be taught? Is the acquisition of knowledge and skills sufficient? Should faculties of education focus on the moral and spiritual formation of teachers? Who should prepare parents and grandparents for the sexual-values education of their children?

Sexuality education does not need new techniques for teaching values, but rather a major shift in paradigm. Sexual-values education will remain inadequate as long as the field holds fast to its epistemological assumptions about the nature of values and valuing, and as long as education continues to be defined and organized according to purely instrumental criteria. One of the most fundamental problems facing sexuality educators today may not be teenage pregnancy or even AIDS, but the overly instrumental and subjectivistic view of values and sexuality education that presently pervades the field. The crisis, in other words, is a crisis in perception and philosophy.

BIBLIOGRAPHY

Ackerman, D. (1990). *A natural history of the senses.* New York: Vintage Books.

Alexander, S. J. (1984). Improving sexual education programs for young adolescents: Parents' views. *Family Relations, 33,* 251-257.

Arendt, H. (1958). *The human condition.* Chicago: The University of Chicago Press.

Arioli, D., & Blake, C. (1987). *Condoms are safes.* Montreal: Fay Institute of Human Relations.

Baum, G. (1981). Ecumenical theology: A new approach. *The Ecumenist, 19*(5), 65-78.

Barrett, M. (1990). Selected observations on sex education in Canada. *SIECCAN Journal, 5*(1), 21-31.

Barrett, M. (1991). Sexual health education: Can a new vision avoid repetition of past errors? *SIECCAN Journal, 6*(4), 3-15.

Barry, K. (1979). *Female sexual slavery.* New York: New York University Press.

Benson, H. (1984). *Beyond the relaxation response.* New York: Berkeley Books.

Bernstein, R. J. (1985). *Beyond objectivism and relativism: Science, hermeneutics, and praxis.* Philadelphia: University of Pennsylvania Press.

Bethge, E. (Ed.). (1972). *Dietrich Bonhoeffer: Letters and papers from prison.* New York: Macmillan.

Bettelheim, B. (1977). *The uses of enchantment: The meaning and importance of fairy tales.* New York: Vintage Books.

Blakely, J. (1988). A review of "Storying: The child's articulation of experience through imagination" (unpublished doctoral dissertation). *Phenomenology and Pedagogy, 6*(1), 51-57.

Bloom, A. (1987). *The closing of the American mind.* New York: Simon & Schuster.

Blume, J. (1986). *Letters to Judy: What kids wish they could tell you.* New York: Pocket Books.

Bollerud, K. H., Christopherson, S. B., Frank, E. S. (1990). Girls' sexual choices: Looking for what is right. In C. Gilligan, N. P. Lyons, & T. J. Hanmer (Eds.). *Making connections: The relational worlds of adolescent girls at the Emma Willard school* (pp. 274- 285). Cambridge, Mass.: Harvard University Press.

Bonisteel, R. (1980). *In search of man alive.* Toronto: Collins.

Boyd, D., & Bodgan, D. (1984). Something clarified, nothing of value: A rhetorical critique of Values Clarification. *Educational Theory* 34, 287-300.

Breckon, D., & Sweeney, D. (1978). Use of Value Clarification in venereal disease education. *Journal of School Health*, 48, 181-183.

Brick, P. (1985). Adolescence in perspective: A lifespan approach to sexuality education. *Seminars in Adolescent Medicine*, 1(2), 139-144.

Brick, P. (1987). AIDS forces the issue: Crisis prevention or education in sexuality. *ASCD Curriculum Update*, 29(7), 1-7.

Bruess, C., & Greenberg, J. (1981). *Sex education: Theory and practice.* Belmont, California: Wadsworth Publishing.

Bruner, J. (1986). *Actual minds, possible worlds.* Cambridge, Mass.: Harvard University Press.

Bruner, J. (1987). Life as narrative. *Social Research*, 54(1), 11-32.

Bruner, J. (1990). *Acts of meaning.* Cambridge, Mass.: Harvard University Press.

Byrne, D., & Fisher, W. (Eds.). (1983). *Adolescents, sex and contraception.* Hillsdale, New Jersey: Erlbaum.

Cairns, K. (1990). The greening of sexuality and intimacy. *SIECCAN Newsletter*, 25(2), 2-10.

Calderone, M. S., & Johnson, E. W. (1989). *The family book about sexuality (revised edition).* New York: Harper & Row.

Capra, F. (1983). *The turning point: Science, society, and the rising culture.* Toronto: Bantam Books.

Carter, R. E. (1984). *Dimensions of moral education.* Toronto: University of Toronto Press.

Cohen, S. (1986). *The magic of touch.* New York: Harper & Row.

Coles, R. (1986). *The moral life of children.* Boston: The Atlantic Monthly Press.

Coles, R. (1989). *The call of stories: Teaching and the moral imagination.* Boston: Houghton Mifflin.

Coles, R. (1990). *The Harvard diary.* New York: Crossroad Publishing.

Colton, H. (1983). *Touch therapy.* New York: Kensington.

Conn, W. (1981). *Conscience: Development and self-transcendence.* Birmingham: Religious Education Press.

Conn, W. (1986). *Christian conversion: A developmental interpretation of autonomy and surrender.* New York: Paulist Press.

Cooper, J. (1991). Telling our own stories: The reading and writing of journals or diaries. In C. Witherell & N. Noddings (Eds.). *Stories lives tell: Narrative and dialogue in education* (pp. 96-112). New York: Teachers College Press.

Darling, C. A., & Mabe, A. R. (1989). Analyzing ethical issues in sexual relationships. *Journal of Sex Education and Therapy,* 15, 234-246.

D'Emilio, J., & Freedman, E. B. (1988). *Intimate matters: A history of sexuality in America.* New York: Harper & Row.

De Smedt, M. (1986). *Éloge du silence.* Paris: Albin Michel.

Désaulniers, M.-P. (1981). Un exemple de débat sur les valeurs: L'éducation sexuelle à l'école. In S. Fleury (Ed.). *L'école et les valeurs: Acts du congrès mondial des sciences de l'éducation* (pp. 285-288). Québec: Les Éditions Agence d'Arc.

Désaulniers, M.-P. (1982). Values and Sex Education. *Lumen Vitae,* 38, 309-321.

Dewey, J. (1956). *The child and the curriculum & the school and society.* Chicago: The University of Chicago Press.

Dewey, J. (1959). *Moral principles in education.* New York: Philosophical Library.

Dewey, J. (1963). *Experience and education.* New York: Collier Books.

Dickman, I. (1982). *Winning the battle for sex education.* New York: SIECUS.

Diori, J. A. (1981). Sex, love and justice: A problem of moral education. *Educational Theory,* 31, 225-235.

Diori, J. A. (1985). Contraception, copulation domination, and the theoretical barrenness of sex education literature. *Educational Theory,* 35, 239-254.

Drake, G. V. (1969). *SIECUS: Corrupters of youth.* Tulsa, Oklahoma: Christian Crusade.

Durand, G. (1985). *L'éducation sexuelle.* Montréal: Éditions Fides.

Egan, K. (1986a). *Teaching as storytelling: An alternative approach to teaching and curriculum in the elementary school.* London, Ontario: The Althouse Press.

Egan, K. (1986b). *Individual development and the curriculum.* London: Hutchinson. (Originally published by Oxford University Press under the title "Educational Development.")

Egan, K. (1988). *Primary understanding: Education in early childhood.* New York: Rutledge.

Egan, K., & Nadaner, D. (1988). *Imagination and education.* New York: Teachers College Press.

Erikson, E. (1963). *Childhood and society.* New York: Norton.

Erikson, E. (1964). *Insight and responsibility.* New York: Norton.

Erikson, J. M. (1988). *Wisdom and the senses: The way of creativity.* New York: W. W. Norton.

Foucault, M. (1980). *History of sexuality: An introduction (Vol.1).* New York: Vintage Books.

Foucault, M. (1985). *History of sexuality: The use of pleasure (Vol. 2).* New York: Vintage Books.

Foucault, M. (1986). *History of sexuality: The care of the self (Vol.3).* New York: Pantheon Books.

Fowler, J. (1980). Faith and the structuring of meaning. In J. Fowler & A. Vergote (Eds.). *Toward moral and religious maturity* (pp. 51-85). Morristown, N. J. Silver Burdett.

Francoeur, R. T. (Ed.). (1991). *Taking sides: Clashing views on controversial issues in human sexuality (3rd ed.).* Guilford, Ct.: Dushkin.

Francoeur, R. T. (1991). *Becoming a sexual person (2nd ed.).* New York: Macmillan

French, M. (1985). *Beyond Power: On women, men, and morals.* New York: Ballantine Books.

Friedman, M. (1987). Beyond caring: The de-moralization of gender. In M. Hanen, & K. Nielson (Eds.). *Science, morality & feminist theory* (pp. 87-110). Calgary: The University of Calgary Press.

Friedman, M. S. (1984). *Contemporary psychology: Revealing and obscuring the human.* Pittsburgh: Duquesne University Press.

Gabler, M., & Gabler, N. (1987). Moral relativism on the ropes. *Communication Education* 36(4), 356-361.

Gadamer, H.-G. (1975). *Truth and method* (G. Barden & J. Cumming Trans.). New York: Continuum (Original work published 1960).

Gadamer, H.-G. (1976). *Philosophical hermeneutics* (D. E. Linge Trans.). Berkeley: University of California Press.

Gallup Poll. (1984). *Planned Parenthood Federation of Canada Newsletter,* September, 8-12.

Gay, P. (1984). *The bourgeois experience (volume 1): Education of the senses.* Oxford: Oxford University Press.

Geertz, C. (1983). *Local knowledge: Further essays in interpretive anthropology.* New York: Basic Books.

George, K. D., & Behrendt, A. E. (1985). Research priorities in sex education. *Journal of Sex Education and Therapy,* 11(1), 56-60.

Gilligan, C. (1974). Sexual Dilemmas at the high school level. In M. Calderone (Ed.). *Sexuality and human values: The personal dimension of sexual experience* (pp. 98-110). New York: Association Press.

Gilligan, C. (1977). In a different voice: Women's conception of self and morality. *Harvard Educational Review,* 47, 481-517.

Gilligan, C. (1980). Justice and responsibility: Thinking about real dilemmas of moral conflict and choice. In J. Fowler, & A. Vergotte (Eds.). *Toward moral and religious maturity* (pp. 223-249). Morristown, N. J.: Silver Burdett.

Gilligan, C. (1982). *In a different voice.* Cambridge, Mass.: Harvard University Press.

Gilligan, C. (1988a). Adolescent development reconsidered. In C. Gilligan, J. V. Ward, & J. M. Taylor (Eds.). *Mapping the moral domain: A contribution of women's thinking to psychological theory and education* (pp. vii-xxxix). Cambridge, Mass.: Harvard University Press.

Gilligan, C. (1988b). Remapping the moral domain: New images of self in relationship. In C. Gilligan, J. V. Ward, and J. M. Taylor (Eds.). *Mapping the moral domain: A contribution of women's thinking to psychological theory and education* (pp. 3-19). Cambridge, Mass.: Harvard University Press.

Gilligan, C., Kohlberg, L., Lerner, J, & Belenky, M. (1971). Moral reasoning about sexual dilemmas. In *Technical report of the commission on obscenity and pornography* (pp. 141-174). Washington, D. C.: U. S. Government Printing Office.

Gilgun, J., & Gordon, S. (1983). The role of values in sex education programs. *Journal of Research and Development in Education,* 16(2), 27-33.

Gordon, S. (1981). The case for a moral sex education in the schools. *Journal of School Health,* 51, 214-218.

Gouldner, A. W. (1962). Anti-minotaur: The myth of value-free sociology. *Social Problems,* 9, 199-213.

Gow, K. M. (1980). *Yes Virginia, there is right and wrong.* Toronto: John Wiley & Sons.

Greeley, A. M. (1988). *Sexual intimacy: Love and play.* New York: Warner Books, 1988.

Greenland, C. (1974). What every young doctor should know about sex. *Medical Aspects of Human Sexuality,* 4(11), 5-26.

Guindon, A. (1977). *The sexual language.* Ottawa: University of Ottawa Press.

Guindon, A. (1986). *The sexual creators: An ethical proposal for concerned Christians.* Lanham: University Press of America.

Guindon, A. (1987, May). Sexuality and the integrated person. *Paper presented at the Ontario Family Life Educators' Association 17th Annual Conference,* Toronto, Ontario.

Guindon, A. (1989a). *Le développement moral.* Ottawa: Novalis.

Guindon, A. (1992). *Moral Development, Ethics and Faith.* Ottawa: Novalis.

Guindon, A. (1989b). Mentioning the unmentionables. *Compass,* 7(3), 6-10.

Guindon, A. (1990). La liberté transcendantale à la lumière d'une explication constructiviste de l'option fondamentale. In J.-C. Petit & J.-C. Breton (Eds.). *Questions de liberté* (pp. 197-230). Montréal: Fides.

Guindon, A. (1991). Une morale pour aujourd'hui est-elle possible? *Revue Notre-Dame,* 11, 1-13.

Harmin, M. (1988). Value clarity, high morality: Let's go for both. *Educational Leadership,* 45(8), 23-30.

Harmin, M., Kirschenbaum, H., & Simon, S. (1973). *Clarifying values through subject matter.* Toronto: Holt, Rinehard & Wilson.

Hauerwas, S. (1977). *Truthfulness and tragedy.* Notre Dame: University of Notre Dame Press.

Hauerwas, S. (1980). Character, narrative, and growth in Christian life. In J. Fowler, (Ed.), *Toward moral and religious maturity.* (pp. 441-484). New Jersey: Silver Burdett Company.

Heidegger, M. (1962). *Being and time.* London: SCM Press.

Herold, E. (1984). *Sexual behavior of Canadian young people.* Markham, Ontario: Fitzhenry & Whiteside.

Hesse, M. (1980). *Revolutions and reconstructions in the philosophy of science.* Brighton, England: Harvester Press.

Howard, M. (1983, March). Postponing sexual involvement: A new approach. *SIECUS Report,* 5-8.

Howard, M.   (1985).   Postponing sexual involvement among adolescents: An alternative approach to prevention of sexually transmitted diseases. *Journal of Adolescent Health Care, 6*, 271-277.

Howard, M. (1990). *Postponing sexual involvement: An educational series for young teens.* Atlanta: Georgia: Emory/Grady Teen Services Program.

Jackson, S. (1982). *Childhood and sexuality.* Oxford: Basil Blackwell.

Jagger, A. M. (1983). *Feminist politics and human nature.* Sussex: The Harvester Press.

Johnson, M. (1993). *Moral Imagination: Implications of Cognitive Science for Ethics.* Chicago: University of Chicago Press.

Jones, E. F., et al.   (1986). *Teenage pregnancy in industrialized countries.* New Haven: Yale University Press.

Karmel, L. (1970). Sex education, no; Sex information, yes. *Phi Delta Kappan, 52*, 95-96.

Keen, S. (1969). *Apology for wonder.* New York: Harper & Row.

Keen, S. (1970). *To a dancing God.* New York: Harper & Row.

Keen, S. (1988, December). The stories we live by. *Psychology Today,* 43-47.

Keen, S.   (1991).   *Fire in the belly: On being a man.*   New York: Bantam Books.

Keen, S., & Valley-Fox, A. (1989).   *Your mythic journey: Finding meaning in your life through writing and storytelling.* Los Angeles: Jeremy P. Tarcher.

Kegan, R. (1970). The seventh grader as artist. *Independent School Bulletin, 29*(4), 28-30.

Kegan, R.   (1977).   *The sweeter welcome: Martin Buber, Bernard Malamud and Saul Bellow.* Needham Heights, Mass.: Wexford.

Kegan, R. (1979). The evolving self: A process conception for ego psychology. *Counselling Psychologist, 8*(2), 5-34.

Kegan, R.   (1980).   There the dance is: Religious dimensions of development theory. In J. Fowler and A. Vergotte (Eds.). *Toward moral and religious maturity* (pp. 403-430). Morristown, New Jersey: Silver Burdett.

Kegan, R. (1982). *The evolving self: Problem and process in human development.* Cambridge, Mass.: Harvard University Press.

Keller, E. F. (1985). *Reflections on gender and science.* New Haven: Yale University Press.

Kelly, G. F. (Ed.). (1985). Sex education: Past, present, future [Special issue]. *Journal of Sex Education and Therapy,* 11(1).

Kelly, G. F. (1988). *Sexuality today: The human perspective.* Gruford, Conn.: Dushkin.

Kenniston, K., et al. (1977). *All our children (The Carnegie Council on children).* New York: Harcourt Brace Jovanovich.

Kenny, A., & Orr, M. T. (1984). Sex Education: An overview of current programs, policies, and research. *Phi Delta Kappan,* 65, 491-96.

King, A., et al. (1988). *Canada youth and AIDS study.* Kingston, Ontario: Queen's University.

Kirby, D. (1980). The effects of school sex education programs, policies, and research. *Phi Delta Kappan,* 65, 559-563.

Kirby, D. (1985). The effects of selected sexuality education programs: Toward a more realistic view. *Journal of Sex Education and Therapy,* 11(1), 28-37.

Kirkendall, L. A. (1981). Sex education in the United States: A historical perspective. In L. Brown (Ed.). *Sex education in the eighties* (pp. 1-18). New York: Plenum Press.

Kirschenbaum, H. (1977). *Advanced value clarification.* La Jolla: University Associates.

Knapp, C. E. (1981). The value of values clarification: A reaction to the critics. *Journal of Environmental Education,* 13(2), 1-4.

Kohlberg, L. (1971, December). The implications of moral stages for problems in sex education. *Paper presented to the Sex Information and Education Council of the United States.*

Kohlberg, L. (1974). Moral stages and sex education. In M. Calderone (Ed.). *Sexuality and human values: The personal dimension of sexual experience* (pp. 111-122). New York: Association Press.

Kohlberg, L. (1975). The cognitive-developmental approach to moral education. *Phi Deta Kappan,* LVI, 670-677.

Kohlberg, L. (1980). Stages of moral development as a basis for moral education. In B. Munsey (Ed.). *Moral development, moral education, and Kohlberg: Basic issues in philosophy, psychology, religion, and education* (pp. 15-98). Birmingham, Al.: Religious Education Press.

Kohlberg, L. (1981). *The philosophy of moral development: Moral stages and the idea of justice.* London: Harper & Row.

Kohlberg, L. (1984). *The psychology of moral development: The nature and validity of moral stages.* San Francisco: Harper & Row.

Kohlberg, L., Levine, C., & Hewer, A. (1983). *Moral stages: A current formulation and a response to the critics.* New York: Karger.

Kuhmerker, L., Gielen, V. P., & Hayes, R. L. (1991). *The Kohlberg legacy for the helping professions.* Birmingham, Al.: Religious Education Press.

Kuhn, T. S. (1970). *The structure of scientific revolutions.* Chicago: The University of Chicago Press.

Lawlor, W., Morris, R., McKay, A., Purcell, L., & Comeau, L. (1990, August/September). Sexuality education and the search for values. *SIECUS Report*, 4-14.

Lawlor, W., & Purcell, L. (1989a). *A study of values and sex education in Montreal area English secondary schools.* Unpublished manuscript, McGill University, Faculty of Education, Montreal.

Lawlor, W., & Purcell, L. (1989b). Values and opinions about sex education among Montreal area English secondary school students. *SIECCAN Journal*, 4(2), 26-33.

Lawlor, W., & Purcell, L. (1990). Parental values and sex education. In S. Dansereau, B. Terrisse, & J.-M. Bouchard (Eds.). *Éducation familiale et intervention précoce* (pp. 246-253). Ottawa: Les édition Agence D'ARC.

Legault, M.-A. (1990, November 18). Nous aussi on veut parler d'amour. *La Presse*, p. A20.

Lentz, G. (1972). *Raping our children.* NewRochelle: Arlington.

Lévi-Strauss, C. (1966). *The savage mind.* Chicago: University of Chicago Press.

Lindbergh, A. M. (1978). *Gift from the sea.* New York: Vintage Books.

Lopez, B. (1990). *Crow and weasal.* San Francisco: North Point Press.

Maguire, D. C. (1978). *The moral choice.* New York: Doubleday.

Marcus, S. (1985). *The other Victorians: A study of sexuality and pornography in mid-nineteenth-century England.* New York: W. W. Norton.

Marchand-Jodoin, L., & Samson, J.-M. (1982). Kohlberg's theory applied to the moral and sexual development of adults. *Journal of Moral Education*, 11, 247-248.

Marsman, J., & Herold, E. S. (1986). Attitudes towards sex education and values in sex education. *Family Relations*, 35, 357-361.

Masters, W. H., & Johnson, V. E. (1975). *The pleasure bond: A new look at sexuality and commitment.* New York: Bantam Press.

Ministry of education. (1985). *Secondary school curriculum: Sex education.* Québec: Government du Québec.

Modgil, S., & Modgil, C. (Eds.). (1986). *Lawrence Kohlberg: Consensus and controversy.* London: Falmer Press.

Monk, E. (1984). Sex education: School yard to school room. *Tellus, Planned Parenthood Federation of Canada Newsletter,* September, 1-6.

Montagu, A. (1971). *Touching: The human significance of the skin.* New York: Columbia University Press.

Moran, G. (1983a). *Religious education development: Images for the future.* Minneapolis, Minnesota: Winston Press.

Moran, G. (1983b). Education: Sexual and religious. In T. Nugent (Ed.), *A challenge to love* (pp. 159-173). New York: Crossroads Publishing.

Moran, G. (1987). *No ladder to the sky: Education and morality.* San Francisco: Harper & Row.

Moran, G. (1989). *Religious education as second language.* Birmingham, Alabama: Religious Education Press.

Morris, R. W. (1986). *Integrating values in sex education.* Journal of Sex Education and Therapy, 12(2), 43-46.

Morris, R. W. (1988). The use and abuse of debating in moral education. *Ethics in Education,* 8(1), 10-11.

Morris, R. W. (1991). Limitations of quantitative methods for research on values in sexuality education. *Canadian Journal of Education,* 16(1), 82-92.

Morrison, E., & Price, M. (1974). *Values in sexuality: A new approach to sex education.* New York: Hart Publishing.

Naus, P. (1989). Sex education re-visited. *SIECCAN Journal,* 4(3), 15-23.

Naus, P. (1991, March). *Some reflections on a new (though not original) way of thinking about sexuality.* Paper presented at the meeting of The Association of Family Life Educators of Quebec, McGill University, Montreal.

Naus, P., & Theis, J. (1991). The construction of sexuality: Implications for sex education and sex therapy. *SIECCAN Journal,* 6(4), 19-24.

Nelson, J. B. (1978). *Embodiment: An approach to sexuality and Christian theology.* Minneapolis, Minn.: Augsburg.

Nelson, J. B. (1988). *The intimate connection: Male sexuality, masculine spirituality.* Philadelphia: Westminster Press.

Niebuhr, R. H. (1963). *The responsible self.* New York: Evanston.

Nielson, K. (1987). Feminist theory - some twistings and turnings. In M. Hanen, & K. Nielson (Eds.). *Science, morality & feminist theory.* (pp. 384-418). Calgary: The University of Calgary Press.

Nolte, J. (1984). Sex education in Canadian classrooms. *Tellus, Planned Parenthood Federation of Canada Newsletter.* September, 13-15.

Nouwen, H. J. (1975). *Reaching out: The three movements of spiritual life.* New York: Doubleday.

Palmer, P. J. (1983). *To know as we are known: A spirituality of education.* San Francisco: Harper & Row.

Palmer, P. J. (1990). *The active life: A spirituality of work, creativity, and caring.* San Francisco: Harper & Row.

Parcel, G. S., & Gordon, S. (Eds.). (1981). Sex education and the public schools [Special Issue]. *Journal of School Health,* 50, 203-316.

Parcel, G. S., Luttman, D., & Flaherty-Zonis, C. (1985). Development and evaluation of a sex education curriculum for young adolescents. *Journal of Sex Education and Therapy,* 11(1), 38-45.

Pearce, J. C. (1986). *The magical child matures.* Toronto: Bantam Books.

Pegis, J., Gentles, I, & de Veber, L. (1986). *Sex Education: a review of the literature from Canada, the United States, Britain and Sweden.* (Report no. 5). Toronto, Ontario: Human Life Research Institute of Ottawa.

Peshkin, A. (1988). In search of subjectivity - one's own. *Educational Researcher,* 17(7), 17-21.

Piaget, J. (1948). *The moral judgment of the child.* Glencoe, Ill.: Free Press.

Piaget, J. (1954). *The construction of reality in the child.* New York: Basic Books.

Piaget, J. (1968). *Six psychological studies.* New York: Vintage Books.

Piaget, J. (1970). *Genetic epistemology.* New York: Columbia University Press.

Piaget, J. (1976). *To understand is to invent.* New York: Penguin Books.

Polakow, V. (1986). On meaningmaking and stories: Young children's experiences with texts. *Phenomenology and Pedagogy,* 4(3), 37-47.

Polanyi, M. (1958). *Personal knowledge.* Chicago: University of Chicago Press.

Polkinghorne, D. (1988). *Narrative knowing and the human sciences.* Albany: SUNY Press.

Postman, N. (1989, December). *Learning by story*. The Atlantic, pp. 119-124.

Power, D. (1980). Some pedagogical methods of sex education (pp. 410-413). In Samson, J.-M. (Ed.). *Enfance et sexualité*. Montréal: Éditions Études Vivantes.

Prescott, J. (1975). Body pleasure and the origins of violence. *The Futurist*, 9(2), 64-74.

Prescott, J. (1989). Affectional bonding for the prevention of violent behaviors: Neurobiological, psychological, and religious/spiritual determinants. In L. J. Hertzberg et al. (Eds.). *Violent behavior, Volume 1: Assessment and Intervention*. New York: PMA Publishing.

Raths, L., Harmin, M., & Simon, S. (1978). *Values and teaching*. Columbus, Ohio: Merril.

Rawls, J. (1971). *A theory of justice*. Cambridge, Mass.: Harvard University Press.

Read, D. A., Simon, S. B, & Goodman J. B. (1977). *Health Education: The Search for Values*. Englewood Cliffs, N.J.: Prentice Hall.

Reimer, J., Paolitto, D., & Hersh, R. (1983). *Promoting moral growth: From Piaget to Kohlberg*. New York: Longman.

Richert, C. (1983). Sex education scandal: How public schools promote promiscuity. In B. Leone & M. T. O'Neill (Eds.). *Sexual values: Opposing viewpoints* (pp. 54-58). St. Paul, Minnesota: Greenhaven Press.

Robb, C. S. (1985). A framework for feminist ethics. In B. H. Andolsen, C. E. Gudorf, & M. D. Pellauer (Eds.). *Women's consciousness, women's conscience* (pp. 211-234). San Francisco: Harper & Row.

Robbins, J. (1987). *Diet for a new America*. Walpole, NH: Stillpoint.

Rogers, W. (1980). Interdisciplinary approaches to moral and religious development. In J. Fowler & A. Vergotte (Eds.). *Toward moral and religious maturity* (pp. 12-50). Morristown, N. J.: Silver Burdett.

Rubin, I. (1968). The importance of moral codes. In I. Rubin & L. Kirkendall (Eds.). *Sex in adolescent years: New direction in guiding and teaching youths* (pp. 111-114). New York: Association Press.

Samson, J.-M. (1978, January). *L'efficacité à long terme d'une intervention structurée d'éducation sexuelle à l'adolescence, conduite selon la pédagogie du +1 de la théorie de L. Kohlberg*.

Montréal: Université du Québec à Montréal, département de sexologie.

Samson, J.-M. (1979). Sex education and values: Is indoctrination avoidable? In D. B. Cochrane & M. Manely-Casimir (Eds.). *Development of Moral Reasoning: Practical Approaches* (pp. 232-68). New York: Praeger.

Samson, J.-M. (1981). *L'éducation sexuelle à L'École.* Montréal: Guérin.

Samson, J.-M. (1987). Valeurs et valeurs sexuelles au Québec. In P. Fortin (Ed.). *L'ethique à venir* (pp. 453-488). Rimouski: Les Éditions du Groupe de Recherches Éthos.

Scales, P. (1984). *The front lines of sexuality education: A guide to building and maintaining community support.* Santa Cruz, Calif.: Network.

Scheller, M. (1991). On the meaning of plumbing and poverty. *Utne Reader,* 44, 101-103.

Schlafly, P. (1983). What's wrong with sex education. In B. Leone & M. T. O'Neill (Eds.). *Sexual values: Opposing viewpoints* (pp. 44-49). St. Paul, Minnesota: Greenhaven Press.

Schlossman, S., & Wallach, S. (1978). The crime of precocious sexuality: Female juvenile delinquency in the Progressive era. *Harvard Education Review,* 48, 65-94.

Schrader, D. (Ed.). (1990). *The legacy of Lawrence Kohlberg.* San Francisco: Jossey-Bass.

Sedway, M. (1992). Far right takes aim at sexuality education. *SIECUS Report,* 20(3), 13-19.

Sex Information and Education Council of the United States. (1970). *Sexuality and man.* New York: Charles Scribner's Sons.

Sexuality Education Study. (1990, January). *SIECUS Report,* 25-27.

SIECUS Position Statements. (1990, January). *SIECUS Report,* 10-13.

Stayton, W. (1985). Religion and adolescent sexuality. *Seminars in Adolescent Medicine,* 1, 131-138.

Storr, A. (1988). *The school of genius.* London: André Deutsch.

Szasz, T. (1980). *Sex by prescription.* New York: Penguin Books.

Tappan, M., & Brown, L. M. (1991). In C. Witherell & N. Noddings (Eds.). *Stories lives tell: Narrative and dialogue in education* (pp. 171-192). New York: Teachers College Press.

Tatum, M. L. (1981). Sex education in the public schools. In L. Brown (Ed.). *Sex education in the eighties* (pp. 137-144). New York: Plenum Press.

Taylor, C. (1991). *The malaise of modernity.* Concord, Ont.: Anansi.

Tracy, D. (1986). *The analogical imagination: Christian theology and the culture of pluralism.* New York: Crossroad.

Trudell, B. K. (1985). The first organized campaign for school sex education: A source of critical questions about current efforts. *Journal of Sex Education and Therapy,* 11(1), 10-15.

Varcoe, C. J. (1988). Sex education: Schools and values. In A. R. Cavaliere & J. M. Riggs (Eds.). *Selected topics in human sexuality* (pp. 161-171). Lanham: University Press of America.

Vreeke, G. J. (1991). Gilligan on justice and care: Two interpretations. *Journal of Moral Education,* 20(1), 33-46.

Witherell, C. S. (1991). Narrative and the moral realm: Tales of caring and justice [special issue]. *Journal of Moral Education,* 20(3), 237-241.

Zukav, G. (1979). *The dancing Wu Li masters.* New York: Bantam Books.

Zullo, J., & Whitehead, J. (1983). The christian body and homosexual maturing. In R. Nugent (Ed.). *A challenge to love* (pp. 20-37). New York: Crossroads.

INDEX

.